G000294264

POWERP
FOR WINDOWS®
FOR
DUMMIES®

Quick Reference

by Camille McCue

IDG
BOOKS
WORLDWIDE™

IDG Books Worldwide, Inc.
An International Data Group Company

Foster City, CA ✦ Chicago, IL ✦ Indianapolis, IN ✦ New York, NY

PowerPoint® 97 For Windows® For Dummies® Quick Reference

Published by
IDG Books Worldwide, Inc.
An International Data Group Company
919 E. Hillsdale Blvd.
Suite 400
Foster City, CA 94404
www.idgbooks.com (IDG Books Worldwide Web site)
www.dummies.com (Dummies Press Web site)

Library of Congress Catalog Card No.: 98-88838

ISBN: 0-7645-0494-0

Printed in the United States of America

10 9 8 7 6 5 4 3 2 1

1P/RQ/RS/ZY/IN

Distributed in the United States by IDG Books Worldwide, Inc.

Distributed by Macmillan Canada for Canada; by Transworld Publishers Limited in the United Kingdom; by IDG Norge Books for Norway; by IDG Sweden Books for Sweden; by Woodslane Pty. Ltd. for Australia; by Woodslane (NZ) Ltd. for New Zealand; by Addison Wesley Longman Singapore Pte Ltd. for Singapore, Malaysia, Thailand, and Indonesia; by Norma Comunicaciones S.A. for Colombia; by Intersoft for South Africa; by International Thomson Publishing for Germany, Austria and Switzerland; by Distribuidora Cuspide for Argentina; by Livraria Cultura for Brazil; by Ediciencia S.A. for Ecuador; by Ediciones ZETA S.C.R. Ltda. for Peru; by WS Computer Publishing Corporation, Inc., for the Philippines; by Contemporanea de Ediciones for Venezuela; by Express Computer Distributors for the Caribbean and West Indies; by Micronesia Media Distributor, Inc. for Micronesia; by Grupo Editorial Norma S.A. for Guatemala; by Chips Computadoras S.A. de C.V. for Mexico; by Editorial Norma de Panama S.A. for Panama; by Wouters Import for Belgium; by American Bookshops for Finland. Authorized Sales Agent: Anthony Rudkin Associates for the Middle East and North Africa.

For general information on IDG Books Worldwide's books in the U.S., please call our Consumer Customer Service department at 800-762-2974. For reseller information, including discounts and premium sales, please call our Reseller Customer Service department at 800-434-3422.

For information on where to purchase IDG Books Worldwide's books outside the U.S., please contact our International Sales department at 317-596-5530 or fax 317-596-5692.

For information on foreign language translations, please contact our Foreign & Subsidiary Rights department at 650-655-3021 or fax 650-655-3281.

For sales inquiries and special prices for bulk quantities, please contact our Sales department at 650-655-3200 or write to the address above.

For information on using IDG Books Worldwide's books in the classroom or for ordering examination copies, please contact our Educational Sales department at 800-434-2086 or fax 317-596-5499.

For press review copies, author interviews, or other publicity information, please contact our Public Relations department at 650-655-3000 or fax 650-655-3299.

For authorization to photocopy items for corporate, personal, or educational use, please contact Copyright Clearance Center, 222 Rosewood Drive, Danvers, MA 01923, or fax 978-750-4470.

is a trademark under exclusive license to IDG Books Worldwide, Inc., from International Data Group, Inc.

About the Author

Camille McCue has lived, slept, and breathed PowerPoint throughout most of the 1990s. She first learned to use the ubiquitous little program as a presentation tool for teaching physics via satellite TV to rural kids across the country. While on-air, she challenged her students to stretch their intellectual limits with activities like "build your own boomerang," even though the kids in upstate New York often lost their creations in the snow. Camille landed her teleteaching position after instructing high school mathematics in a farm community south of her hometown of San Antonio, Texas. Prior to that, she worked as a marketing representative — and printer specialist (yawn) — for IBM.

For three exhilarating years, Camille worked for NASA, producing and hosting live electronic field trips showcasing the agency's cutting-edge aerospace research. There, she employed every imaginable telecommunication technology — including satellite, compressed video, microwave, and the Internet — to deliver programming to schools and the public. Since 1993, she has also served as host of the PBS "Passport to Knowledge" project, and was especially thrilled to anchor a live uplink celebrating the 1997 landing of Mars Pathfinder.

Camille absolutely loves her current position as the Ready to Learn program administrator for KLVX-TV, the PBS affiliate in Las Vegas, Nevada. There, she coaches teachers, librarians, and parents in using PBS kids' shows like *Arthur* and *Wishbone* as vehicles for promoting children's literacy.

Camille has an M.A. in Education, with an emphasis in Curriculum and Instruction, from the University of Texas at San Antonio, and a B.A. in Mathematics from the University of Texas at Austin (go Longhorns!). She is a certified teacher in physics and mathematics, and serves as adjunct faculty teaching classroom computer applications at UNLV.

Work aside, Camille is an enthusiastic champion of Las Vegas, an avid devourer of Indian food, and a dedicated fan of *X-Files*. But most of all, she is passionate about her exceptionally wonderful and supportive husband Michael, their two tabby cats, and their three tri-colored beagles.

ABOUT IDG BOOKS WORLDWIDE

Welcome to the world of IDG Books Worldwide.

IDG Books Worldwide, Inc., is a subsidiary of International Data Group, the world's largest publisher of computer-related information and the leading global provider of information services on information technology. IDG was founded more than 25 years ago and now employs more than 8,500 people worldwide. IDG publishes more than 275 computer publications in over 75 countries (see listing below). More than 90 million people read one or more IDG publications each month.

Launched in 1990, IDG Books Worldwide is today the #1 publisher of best-selling computer books in the United States. We are proud to have received eight awards from the Computer Press Association in recognition of editorial excellence and three from *Computer Currents'* First Annual Readers' Choice Awards. Our best-selling *...For Dummies*® series has more than 50 million copies in print with translations in 38 languages. IDG Books Worldwide, through a joint venture with IDG's Hi-Tech Beijing, became the first U.S. publisher to publish a computer book in the People's Republic of China. In record time, IDG Books Worldwide has become the first choice for millions of readers around the world who want to learn how to better manage their businesses.

Our mission is simple: Every one of our books is designed to bring extra value and skill-building instructions to the reader. Our books are written by experts who understand and care about our readers. The knowledge base of our editorial staff comes from years of experience in publishing, education, and journalism — experience we use to produce books for the '90s. In short, we care about books, so we attract the best people. We devote special attention to details such as audience, interior design, use of icons, and illustrations. And because we use an efficient process of authoring, editing, and desktop publishing our books electronically, we can spend more time ensuring superior content and spend less time on the technicalities of making books.

You can count on our commitment to deliver high-quality books at competitive prices on topics you want to read about. At IDG Books Worldwide, we continue in the IDG tradition of delivering quality for more than 25 years. You'll find no better book on a subject than one from IDG Books Worldwide.

IDG BOOKS WORLDWIDE

John Kilcullen
John Kilcullen
CEO
IDG Books Worldwide, Inc.

Steven Berkowitz
Steven Berkowitz
President and Publisher
IDG Books Worldwide, Inc.

VIII
WINNER

Eighth Annual
Computer Press
Awards ≥1992

IX
WINNER

Ninth Annual
Computer Press
Awards ≥1993

Tenth Annual
Computer Press
Awards ≥1994

X
WINNER

XI
WINNER

Eleventh Annual
Computer Press
Awards ≥1995

Dedication

To Michael and Mom.

Author's Acknowledgments

I'd like to thank former Acquisitions Editor Darlene Wong who accepted my first phone call to IDG, and Editorial Manager Mary Corder who explained "the business" over a Las Vegas breakfast buffet at the Stratosphere. I'd also like to thank ...*For Dummies* author Michelle Robinette for her insightful advice on undertaking this venture (and for her great books which I teach with frequently!).

Thanks are especially due to my patient and efficient Project Editor, Colleen Esterline, who caught this hot potato of a project and brought it to fruition with expert skill — and only a little cracking of the whip. I hope I have the good fortune of working with her again in the future.

I would also like to express my thanks to Diane Giangrossi for her tireless editing of my work; Stephanie Koutek for fixing all my grammatical boo-boos; and Allen Wyatt for going over the technical details of this little book with a fine-tooth comb. My hat is off to them all.

Lastly I would like to acknowledge Acquisitions Editor Steve Hayes and Project Editor Mary Goodwin for negotiating the many logistical issues associated with making this book finally happen. I appreciate their diligence, business-savvy, and kindness.

Publisher's Acknowledgments

We're proud of this book; please register your comments through our IDG Books Worldwide Online Registration Form located at: http://my2cents.dummies.com.

Some of the people who helped bring this book to market include the following:

Acquisitions, Editorial, and Media Development

Project Editor:
Colleen Williams Esterline

Acquisitions Editor: Steven H. Hayes

Copy Editors: Diane Giangrossi,
Stephanie Koutek

Technical Editors: Allen Wyatt,
Discovery Computing, Inc.

Editorial Assistant: Donna Love

Production

Project Coordinator: Regina Snyder

Layout and Graphics: Lou Boudreau,
J. Tyler Connor, Maridee V. Ennis,
Angela F. Hunckler, Brent Savage,
Michael A. Sullivan

Proofreaders: Christine Berman,
Kelli Botta, Sarah Fraser,
Rebecca Senninger, Ethel M. Winslow,
Janet M. Withers

Indexer: Anne Leach

Special Help Mary Corder,
Mary Goodwin, Patricia Yuu Pan,
Kathleen Dobie

General and Administrative

IDG Books Worldwide, Inc.: John Kilcullen, CEO; Steven Berkowitz, President and Publisher

IDG Books Technology Publishing: Brenda McLaughlin, Senior Vice President and Group Publisher

Dummies Technology Press and Dummies Editorial: Diane Graves Steele, Vice President and Associate Publisher; Mary Bednarek, Director of Acquisitions and Product Development; Kristin A. Cocks, Editorial Director

Dummies Trade Press: Kathleen A. Welton, Vice President and Publisher; Kevin Thornton, Acquisitions Manager

IDG Books Production for Dummies Press: Michael R. Britton, Vice President of Production and Creative Services; Cindy L. Phipps, Manager of Project Coordination, Production Proofreading, and Indexing; Kathie S. Schutte, Supervisor of Page Layout; Shelley Lea, Supervisor of Graphics and Design; Debbie J. Gates, Production Systems Specialist; Robert Springer, Supervisor of Proofreading; Debbie Stailey, Special Projects Coordinator; Tony Augsburger, Supervisor of Reprints and Bluelines

Dummies Packaging and Book Design: Robin Seaman, Creative Director; Kavish + Kavish, Cover Design

♦

The publisher would like to give special thanks to Patrick J. McGovern, without whom this book would not have been possible.

♦

Contents at a Glance

Table of Contents

How to Use This Book

Imagine giving your next presentation with dynamic graphics, crisp text, snazzy sounds, and awesome animation. Now imagine not having to stay up all night — or not paying a Fort Knox fortune — to create that presentation! That's what PowerPoint is all about: creating high-impact presentations with minimal bother. Most importantly, you won't require a four-credit college course to master PowerPoint. All you need is this *PowerPoint 97 For Windows For Dummies Quick Reference* — the perfect guide for answering your PowerPoint "how-do-I?"s. No fuss. No boring details; just quick answers to your questions about using the coolest presentation program ever, PowerPoint.

How This Book Is Organized

This quick reference is divided into several parts for easy search-and-find PowerPoint missions. Within each part, topics are organized alphabetically, and each topic is usable as a standalone unit. Don't feel compelled to start on page 1, moving page by page until you reach the "z" entries in the Glossary. Allow yourself to bypass all material not pertaining directly to the information you seek . . . after all, this is a quick reference!

The following parts describe the arrangement of material within this book:

Part I: Getting to Know PowerPoint

If you peruse nothing more than this part, you'll still be revered as a PowerPoint smarty-pants among your peers. This part overviews the basic features of PowerPoint and gives you a preliminary road map for navigating through the program. You'll find out what functions are performed by toolbars and buttons, and how to go about building and looking at your presentations from several available views. Additionally, Part I addresses how to move among different versions of PowerPoint.

Part II: Quickstart: Creating a Presentation

Part II covers the basic steps involved in building and showing a PowerPoint presentation. From working with hand-holding wizards and preformatted templates to stark-naked blank setups, this part initiates the presentation development process. Part II also shows you how to add new slides, format the slides using AutoLayouts and color schemes, and move among multiple slides in a presentation.

Part III: Laying the Groundwork: Working with Templates and Masters

This part addresses the nuts and bolts of setting up the blueprint from which your presentation of PowerPoint slides is built. Here, you'll find tips on selecting, editing, and applying templates that prescribe the aesthetic look of all slides in a presentation. Part III also includes information on manipulating the master documents that dictate the structure of slides, the title slide, audience handouts, and speaker notes.

Part IV: Adding Text

Writing words and sentences on slides is the task you'll probably perform most frequently in PowerPoint, and this part serves as your reference for adding all such text information. Here, you'll find details on creating and formatting text, including: font selection, changing text colors, bulleting, bolding and italicizing, spell-checking, finding and replacing text, and setting indents and tabs. Part IV also shows how to create three-dimensional text using the WordArt program.

Part V: Drawing Your Own Graphics

For those of you not content with mere text and lovely backgrounds, Part V explores how you can add real panache to your stash of slides. This part gives the lowdown on using PowerPoint's basic drawing tools to add simple graphic elements to your slides. It also covers more advanced drawing features, such as using AutoShapes, filling, grouping, layering, drawing and formatting lines and polygons, rotating, and shadowing.

Part VI: Adding Multimedia Goodies

This part examines how to incorporate the bedazzling media of sounds and movies to spice up your slides and increase information-delivery. Don't miss this part if you're looking for simple ways to use the "pretty media." Part VI addresses how to embellish your presentations with clip art and picture images, sound, and video. This part also provides guidance in selecting the right file formats when adding such goodies to your presentation.

Part VII: Showing Your Business Savvy

Part VII deals with using PowerPoint tools that help you visually express analytical data, procedures, and relationships — the stuff of every good business presentation! You'll find information on how to build organizational charts to show relationships among entities or explain step-by-step processes. Additionally, this part covers how to convert numerical information into snappy-looking graphs in every conceivable format from bar graphs to pie charts.

Part VIII: Showing the Presentation

This part helps you with putting the finishing touches on a slide show to make it ready for audience presentation. It provides details on manipulating the "performance look" of your presentation, such as establishing how your slides are sequenced and the order and pace at which slide information is presented. Nifty animation features are explained, like how to make individual lines of text zip across the screen as each new point is revealed, and how to use slide transitions to remove and reveal slides. This part also covers creating action buttons and hyperlinks for gaining nonlinear control over your formal presentation. Lastly, Part VIII addresses the physical equipment needed to display your presentation to large and small audiences, in face-to-face settings, and on the World Wide Web.

Part IX: Publishing the Presentation

This part assists you with packaging your PowerPoint presentation in a variety of distribution formats. You find everything you need to know about generating on-screen shows, 35mm slides, and color and black-and-white transparencies. You can also find information on creating hardcopy printouts of slides used in your presentation — a simple and sharp-looking way to create audience handouts. Part IX also shows the techies among you how to convert your PowerPoint presentation into HTML so that it can be shown online via the web.

Part X: Tips, Tricks, and Troubleshooting

Part X addresses all the necessary issues that accompany working with PowerPoint. Assorted odds and ends such as file management and time-saving tips are covered in the part. You'll also find problem-solving strategies for figuring out solutions to PowerPoint mysteries and presentations gone bad.

Glossary: Techie Talk

Every discipline has its own unique jargon, and the world of technology is no different. Because PowerPoint's special list of vocabulary will occasionally cause you to scratch your head dumbfoundedly, I'm including a handy glossary called "Techie Talk" at the back of this book.

Conventions Used in This Book

While you're reading through the book, you may notice strange symbols that imitate Egyptian hieroglyphics, such as

File⇨New

This sentence with the arrow tells you to click File on the main menu and then click New from the drop-down menu.

You may also see little lines under certain letters (check out the preceding example). These hotkeys give you a quick way to get the same thing accomplished. When you see one, press the Alt key to make the menu come up and then type the underlined letter to pick a menu item.

Terms are alphabetized for easy retrieval. Just remember — mastery of such terms will delight and impress your friends.

Icons Used in This Book

Much like the autobahn in Germany, it's a good idea to post universally accepted road signs to guide your quick travel down the PowerPoint highway. I know you plan on flipping fast and furious through the following pages, and these handy icons will help focus your attention as you navigate to the information you seek.

This quick reference offers the following icons as guidance:

The Tip icon points you to special information that will make your life much easier.

The Warning icon alerts you to potential PowerPoint disasters that can ruin your presentation. Think, "Danger, Will Robinson!"

The Cross-Reference icon sends you to another Dummies Press book if you need extra guidance or information.

The Fast Track icon informs you of the most expedient way to accomplish a task. Often, this is a keystroke combination or toolbar button.

The Weirdness icon says, "Yes, I know this procedure seems illogical and counterintuitive, but this is how Microsoft set up this silly program anyway."

Part 1

Getting to Know PowerPoint

Say goodbye to dreary ol' presentation media like whiteboards and viewgraphs. Say hello to ultra-professional looking PowerPoint visuals built in bodacious colors and embellished with eye-popping text, graphics, charts, and movies! I'll help you integrate terms like *new slide* and *insert sound* into your daily vocabulary, and assist you in keeping record numbers of coworkers awake during the next staff meeting.

In this part . . .

- ✔ **Defining PowerPoint**
- ✔ **Opening a PowerPoint presentation**
- ✔ **Using buttons and bars**
- ✔ **Changing views**
- ✔ **Getting help**
- ✔ **Saving your work**
- ✔ **Closing a presentation**
- ✔ **Exiting PowerPoint**

What Is PowerPoint?

PowerPoint is software that lets you create professional-looking presentations using your personal computer. After creating the presentation, PowerPoint then gives you several ways of showing the presentation to your intended audience. You can display your wares using everything from computer monitors to overhead transparencies to slickly formatted handouts. The software is cheap, the creation time is minimal, and the results are powerful (I guess that's why they named it *Power*Point!).

What Is a Slide?

PowerPoint images have their own special terminology: they're called *slides*. And in many ways, your audiences will view PowerPoint slides in similar fashion to the way they view regular 35mm slides projected from a slide carousel. But making and showing PowerPoint slides is much easier, much faster, and much more functional than regular ol' slides.

Showing PowerPoint slides is also much more exciting than clicking through traditional slides. That's because a PowerPoint presentation can include animated text and graphics, video, and audio clips. It can also include television-quality cuts and fades between slides. Keep in mind that you'll usually show PowerPoint slides directly from a notebook or desktop computer — a major technological advantage over using low-end devices like overhead projectors or slide carousels.

So what does a PowerPoint slide actually look like? Sometimes it looks like a simple piece of text like your company mission statement. Other times it looks like a list of bullet items like ingredients for guacamole. And other times it looks like a graph of product sales forecasts or a labeled diagram of earthworm innards. If you can dream it up, you can probably stick it on a slide and show it to your audience.

Starting PowerPoint and Opening a Presentation

1. Turn on your computer.

2. Click the Start button, click Programs⇨Microsoft PowerPoint.

Your computer is now starting up the PowerPoint program. Wait patiently. After PowerPoint boots up you'll see the start-up dialog box.

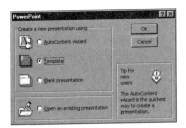

The start-up dialog box provides four choices to begin developing your PowerPoint presentation:

✦ **<u>A</u>utoContent wizard:** The wizard yields a near-complete prefabricated set of PowerPoint slides. You just need to supply the wizard some basic lines of text, let the wizard do its thing, and then you can tweak the final product.

✦ **<u>T</u>emplate:** This option provides you cool predesigned layouts that still offer you the flexibility to alter the layout elements.

✦ **<u>B</u>lank presentation:** Gives you blank slides with no color and no artwork, which is great for the minimalists and artists. Allows you to build a really barren stack of slides (good for black and white transparencies), or else create all your artistic elements from scratch.

✦ **<u>O</u>pen an existing presentation:** Lets you go back and work on slide stacks you've not yet completed.

See also Part II for more information about using these options.

Moving Around in PowerPoint 97

PowerPoint, like most every other Windows program, makes use of assorted methods in getting you through the process of building and showing a presentation. You input information through the keyboard and the mouse, and you define your presentation's parameters using menus, dialog boxes, and toolbar buttons.

Using the keyboard

The keyboard attached to your computer probably looks and functions much the same way as a trusty old typewriter, with a couple of exceptions. Besides not having to bang the keys with finger-exhausting power, your computer keyboard also offers extra keys which provide a variety of helpful functions. Here's a sampling of what you can do with your keyboard:

Key	Action it Performs
Esc	Backs you out of menu or dialog box commands, and halts a slide show in progress
F1-F12	Provides shortcut functions for a variety of menu commands
Delete	Cuts the currently highlighted text, the selected object, or the character to the right of the cursor
Home	Takes you to the first slide in your presentation, in any view
End	Takes you to the last slide in your presentation, in any view
Insert	Toggles between inserting and overstriking (replacing) characters while you edit text
PgUp	Takes you one slide back in your presentation, in any view
PgDn	Takes you one slide forward in your presentation, in any view
Left, up arrows	Moves you one animation step backward in your presentation in slide show view only
Right, down arrows	Moves you one animation step forward in your presentation in slide show view only

Using the mouse

The kidney-shaped plastic device tethered to your computer is known as a mouse. The mouse serves to operate the on-screen pointer which is used for selecting objects, moving them around and other necessary activities.

When you look on your screen, you'll notice a pointer that indicates your position on-screen and changes shape depending on the job it's available to perform. When the pointer appears as an arrow, you can use it to select something. When it appears as a double-headed arrow, you can use it to resize something. And when it appears as an I-beam, you can use the pointer to type or edit text.

The mouse itself has two buttons, one on the left and another on the right. Much of the time you will click one of these buttons or click and hold a button as you drag the mouse over the mousepad. Sometimes you will need to double-click the mouse, which means to click the left button two times in rapid succession. You may want to start muscling-up your right index finder as you'll find you spend significantly more time left-clicking and doubling-clicking than right-clicking.

Working with dialog boxes

PowerPoint often presents little interactive windows called dialog boxes. A dialog box appears as the result of certain commands you execute, and offers additional options which refine exactly how you want the command performed. You must respond to queries posed by the box before you can continue working.

The following dialog box is similar to many you will find in PowerPoint. This one shows the Page Setup dialog box, which pops up when you choose File⇨Page Setup from the Menu bar. Notice that the dialog box always appears on top of other on-screen work areas.

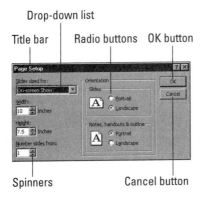

Drop-down list

Title bar   Radio buttons   OK button

Spinners   Cancel button

Following is a list of parts you'll find staring back at you from a typical dialog box:

- ✦ **Title bar:** Reminds you of which dialog box you're operating.

- ✦ **Help button:** Links you with help tools that offer further assistance in completing information requested in the box.

- ✦ **Command button:** Performs an action when pressed. A button showing an ellipsis opens another dialog box when pressed.

- ✦ **Spinner:** An up/down pair of small arrow buttons that allows you to increase or decrease the value shown in the spinner box. Alternatively, you can type a value in the box.

- ✦ **Drop-down list:** A list that drops down from a window whenever you press the down arrow next to the window. Click and hold on the arrow and drag the mouse to an item on the list to select it.

- ✦ **Radio button:** Allows you to select only one of the items in the group. Click in the white circle to choose your selection.

✦ **Cancel button:** Causes the dialog box to vanish, with no action taken.

✦ **OK button:** Closes the dialog box and executes the selections made in the box.

You can move around a dialog box simply by clicking the area to which you want to go. You can also move rapidly from one area to the next by pressing the Tab key.

Working with windows

Windows allow you to determine how much area on-screen each open program occupies. You have the option of sizing your PowerPoint window to take up part of the screen or all of the screen, or you can reduce the program to a mere button on the taskbar. You also have the option of sizing each individual presentation file you open in PowerPoint. Upon closing PowerPoint, its program windows disappear from on-screen without a trace.

Three little buttons in the upper-right corner of the PowerPoint window govern the sizing of the program window:

 ✦ **Minimize button:** Clicking this button reduces PowerPoint to a single button on the taskbar at the bottom of the screen. Clicking a minimized taskbar button restores the program's window on-screen.

 ✦ **Maximize button:** Clicking this button causes PowerPoint to occupy the entire on-screen area.

 ✦ **Restore button:** Clicking this button causes PowerPoint to occupy a sizable window on-screen. You can click and drag on the title bar of the restored window to move its location. You can also click and drag the edge or corner of a restored window to resize it.

Using Buttons and Bars

Like most Windows-based programs, you operate PowerPoint using a handful of buttons and toolbars. Most of the time you view the buttons and bars as they appear in slide mode — the mode that lets you see each slide under construction.

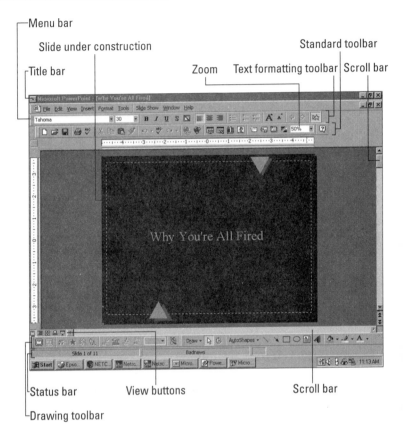

Menu bar

Slide under construction

Title bar

Zoom   Text formatting toolbar   Scroll bar

Standard toolbar

Status bar   View buttons   Scroll bar

Drawing toolbar

If you have ever used computer software in your life (at least in the post-DOS years), I'll bet that many of these buttons and bars look familiar to you. Here's a quick tour of the many buttons and bars available for your use:

✦ **Title bar:** Tells you the name of the presentation you're working on, like *Pop Pigs* or *Why You're all Fired*. The title appears at the very top of the screen.

✦ **Menu bar:** Sits just below the title bar in Windows. It allows you to control the basic functions of the PowerPoint program.

✦ **Toolbars:** Offer you buttons for some of the most commonly used operations from the menus on the menu bar.

• *Standard toolbar:* Features frequently used actions such as save, print, spell-check, and zoom.

• *Text Formatting and Drawing toolbars:* Help you put words and pictures on your slides.

• *Common Tasks toolbar:* Puts your three most frequently used operations (adding a new slide, choose a slide layout, and choosing a slide design) in one easily-accessible spot.

The first time you open PowerPoint in Windows, you'll see the Common Tasks toolbar in a box in the middle of the screen — just grab the top of the box and drag it to the bottom-right corner of the screen.

✦ **Scroll bars:** Two scroll bars border the slide work area: one on the right and one on the bottom. Pressing the arrows at the ends of the scroll bars adjusts your viewing perspective of the slide work area.

✦ **Status bar:** Indicates which slide you're working on at any given time.

✦ **View buttons:** Give you different ways of viewing your PowerPoint slides. We'll talk more about these in a moment.

Still confused about the whole business of buttons and bars? Then tread back to your bookstore and nab a copy of *Windows 95 For Dummies* or *Windows 98 For Dummies*, both by Andy Rathbone (IDG Books Worldwide, Inc.). And call me in the morning.

Changing Your View

Next to the horizontal scrollbar sits a collection of buttons from which you can choose your view. These buttons allow you to build and examine your slides in an assortment of ways. The options provide you everything from a graphic view of a single slide to an outline view of text only on your entire stack of slides. You can also choose a view by clicking the <u>V</u>iew menu from the Menu bar. Here are your viewing options:

 ✦ **Slide view:** Shows a single slide under construction. You'll be able to see all text, colors, pictures, sounds, and movies in the view. This view allows you to create and edit all information and images on your slides. *See also* Part II for more information on working with Slide view.

 ✦ **Outline view:** Shows an ordered list of the text information on your slides. In outline view, you can examine the entire text content of your presentation all at once. This view allows you to create and edit text information on your slides. But it does not let you add or edit non-text items such as clip art. This view also gives you a cute thumbnail sketch of your slide beside its associated outline position. *See also* Part II for more details on working with Outline view.

✦ **Slide Sorter view:** Shows thumbnails of all your slides simultaneously, neatly presented in orderly rows and columns. Slide Sorter View lets you quickly resequence your slides by dragging and dropping them into new positions. *See also* Part VIII.

✦ **Notes Pages view:** Shows a graphic view of the slide accompanied by a block of presenter comments and notes. Presenter notes do not appear visible to your audience watching the slide presentation, but they do print out on hard-copy handouts of the notes pages. *See also* Part IX for more information about working with the Notes Pages view.

✦ **Slide show view:** Presents the completed stack of slides to a viewing audience. *See also* Part VIII.

Getting Help

PowerPoint 97 offers an assortment of handy help tools to aid you through the stumbling blocks along your presentation-building route.

Using the Help menu

PowerPoint provides traditional Help menu features in a Help table of contents. This Help table of contents is called Help Topics: Microsoft PowerPoint, and can be summoned by choosing Help⇨Contents and Index from the menu bar. Help Topics can be perused using three different methods, each one labeled with its own tab. The three Help Topics tabs consist of the following:

✦ **Contents:** Lists all available PowerPoint topics, organized into little *books*. Double-click a topic book to expand chapters of information, and display a chapter by double-clicking it.

✦ **Index:** Provides an alphabetized list of all Help topics. Type the topic you want to search for, and the Help index will take you directly to the topic — if it contains an entry for the topic. Double-click on your chosen topic to display its contents.

✦ **Find:** Creates a searchable database of every word contained in PowerPoint's Help files. The first time you use Find, the Help table of contents builds the find index. After building this find index, PowerPoint asks you to type a word to search for. You're then asked to choose among some alternative words to further define the search. When the specific help topic you desire appears, double-click the topic to display its information.

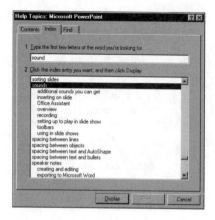

Using the Assistant

The most useful — and also the most playful — help tool takes the form of a tiny cartoon character called the Office Assistant. The Assistant appears in a small window and can easily be turned off — if he gets too feisty — by clicking the X in the upper right-hand corner of his window.

Summon the Assistant using any of these methods:

✦ Choose Help➪Microsoft PowerPoint Help from the menu bar.

✦ Click the Office Assistant button on the Standard toolbar.

✦ Press F1.

Each time you call upon the Assistant, it evaluates what PowerPoint activity you are working on and tries to guess what help you may require. The Assistant then provides a list of possible help topics from which you make a selection — or completely ignore.

The Assistant initially appears as an animated paper clip named Clipit, but you can change it to any of several other characters. My personal favorite is PowerPup. To hire a different Assistant:

1. Open the Assistant by pressing Help⇨Microsoft PowerPoint Help from the menu bar.

2. Click Options to summon the Office Assistant dialog box.

3. Press the Gallery tab.

Browse the Gallery by clicking Next or Back to examine each available Assistant. You are provided many choices from The Dot to Mother Nature to Will (as in Will Shakespeare). When you find an Assistant you like, stop browsing.

4. Click OK to accept your choice of Assistant.

You will find the Assistant helpful not only for responding to help queries you pose, but also for anticipating questions you may have while working in PowerPoint. The Assistant is a good mind reader, and enjoys popping on-screen whenever it thinks you may need a little guidance.

The Office Assistant dialog box offers an Options tab that allows you to fine-tune many details of how and when the Assistant provides help.

Using the Internet

PowerPoint also offers help via the Internet by providing a direct link to Microsoft's Help web site. Although PowerPoint provides several online links, you will most frequently use Help⇨Microsoft on the Web⇨Online Support link from the menu bar. Choosing this help option launches your web browser and transports you directly to Microsoft Help. When you first arrive at the site, you will be asked to complete and submit an online profile. Subsequent visits are more expedient.

Many support features are available from the web site, but you will probably find these areas most worthwhile to visit:

✦ **Search Support Online:** This area is a searchable database of technical information about all of Microsoft's programs, PowerPoint included. Search Support Online serves a similar role as PowerPoint's Help Contents and Index, but the online information is much more comprehensive and up-to-date.

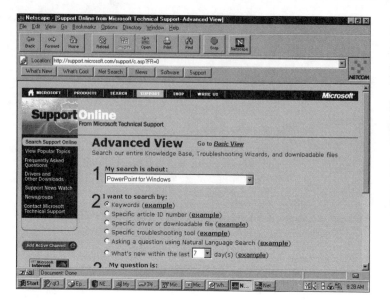

+ **Frequently Asked Questions:** The FAQ area lists and answers the most commonly asked questions about PowerPoint. This is a good place to go if you believe you're asking something that many other people have probably asked at some point.

+ **Newsgroups:** The Newsgroup area provides a Microsoft-sponsored Internet discussion group for PowerPoint. This area is ideal for asking the quirky questions you believe may require an expert to figure out. Simply post a question to the group, and a few hours (or days) later, someone in the know will respond with an answer.

Using the What's This? button

The What's This? button is a nifty little help tool that let's you point to items on-screen and ask, "What's This?" This tool is a quick and easy way to get short answers to many PowerPoint questions without searching through Help menus.

Summon the What's This? button using either of these methods:

+ Choose Help⇨What's This? from the menu bar.

+ Press Shift+F1.

 Your pointer will suddenly sprout a small question mark on its side. Move the pointer to any item on-screen — such as a button on a toolbar — and click. A pop-up box will appear with a brief explanation of the selected item's function or purpose.

Saving Your Work

After composing and printing an award-winning presentation or lecture, you'll certainly want to save your work. Save your goods using one of the following methods:

✦ Click the Save button on the Standard toolbar.

✦ Choose the File⇨Save command.

✦ Press Ctrl+S or Shift+F12.

The first time you save, the Save As dialog box appears for you to type in the name of your newly created file. You also have the option of filling out a very long questionnaire with archive information about your file. This archiving option is located at File ⇨ Properties, and although I usually ignore this option, it can be useful for making your files easier to track down at a later date. After naming your file, click OK.

Save often. If you close your file or exit PowerPoint without saving your slides, consider them gone forever. Saving often also buys you insurance against losing everything in the event you have a power surge or a computer crash.

Closing Up Shop

Now that you've had a successful first encounter with PowerPoint, it's time to close up shop, kick back for the evening, and bask in a little Microsoft glory. Feels good, doesn't it? Close the files with which you've been working as follows:

✦ Use the File⇨Close command.

✦ Press Ctrl+W.

You don't need to use Close if you are going to exit the program. You may instead simply Exit, and the program will save your work and close your presentation as it shuts down.

Exiting PowerPoint

The final step to getting this initial PowerPoint excursion over and done is to exit PowerPoint. Say goodbye using one of these methods:

✦ Choose the File⇨Exit command.

✦ Click the X box at the top right corner of the PowerPoint window.

✦ Press Alt+F4.

PowerPoint won't let you quit without asking if you'd like to save changes. Answer politely to complete the exiting process.

You're on your way!

Moving Between Versions

You can convert a presentation from an older version to a newer version. Just boot up the newest PowerPoint and open your old presentation from inside the File menu. A serious-looking message will appear warning you that the file will be opened as read-only. Finish the update conversion by saving the file with a new name.

Once the file is saved with a new name, it is no longer read-only and you can make changes and resave as needed.

Part II

Quickstart: Creating a Presentation

This part covers the basic steps — start to finish — that you need to create and present a PowerPoint presentation. It won't make you a PowerPoint virtuoso, but it will guide you in performing the basic tasks of generating slides, adding text and pictures, and outputting your presentation in a variety of formats. If you're ready to build a *slide show* — PowerPoint's lingo for presentation — and you don't have time for the fancy stuff of later parts, then this Quickstart is the place for you.

In this part . . .

✔ **Creating your first PowerPoint presentation**

✔ **Test-driving the program**

✔ **Printing — the basics**

✔ **Showing your presentation — more basics**

Beginning a New Presentation

Every time you start the PowerPoint program, a start-up dialog box appears and offers you the option of opening a new presentation. Once at the start-up dialog box, you can begin a new presentation simply by clicking Blank presentation, Template, or AutoContent wizard and then clicking OK.

If you already have PowerPoint up and running, you can use either of these methods to start a new presentation:

✦ Choose File➪New from the menu bar

✦ Press Ctrl+N

You will be presented with a New Presentation dialog box when using these methods to create a new presentation. Don't be surprised that the New Presentation dialog box looks very different from the start-up dialog box.

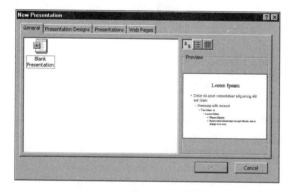

When opening a new PowerPoint presentation, your work area will always appear as the Slide view. If you save a presentation in some other view, such as Outline or Slide Sorter, PowerPoint will re-open the presentation in the view being used at the time of the most recent save.

Creating a blank presentation

Choosing Blank Presentation from the start-up dialog box or the new presentation dialog box provides you blank slides with no color and no artwork.

Blank presentations can still provide placeholders for adding text and graphic objects, but are otherwise barren of images or artistic design. They are ideal for building complete layouts from scratch or for using *as is* to construct overhead transparencies with minimal clutter.

Creating a presentation with templates

Choosing Template from the start-up dialog box or new presentation dialog box means you'll have to shop from a folder full of pretty designs before singling out one that catches your eye.

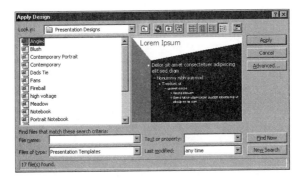

Clicking once the name of any template yields a thumbnail sketch of how the design will appear on your computer screen. Pick a style that suits your fancy and then accept it by clicking OK.

Creating a presentation with the wizard

The wizard serves as a simple program that builds a rudimentary set of PowerPoint slides based on a few tidbits of information you input to the program. The wizard is a good way to get started with PowerPoint, but don't be fooled into thinking that it magically does all the work for you — it won't. Just accept the wizard for what it is — a quick and dirty way to get a basic set of PowerPoint slides generated.

1. Start PowerPoint.

2. At the start-up dialog box, click AutoContent Wizard and click OK.

3. Click Next.

The wizard now initiates a series of query screens.

4. Choose a presentation type from the list, and then click Next.

5. Choose how you will use the presentation, and then click Next.

6. Pick an output option, indicate whether you intend to print handouts and then click Next.

A fill-in-the-blank screen appears for you to supply some earth-shattering information.

7. You are asked for information that is used to construct the title slide of your presentation. In the empty text boxes, type the title of your presentation, your name, and the main discussion points, and then click Next.

The wizard presents a final wrap-up screen.

8. Click Finish.

To make sense of the completed presentation, check out the next sections.

Creating and Working with Slides

Slides are the fundamental building blocks of a PowerPoint presentation. All information in your presentation either appears directly on the slide or is attached to the slide as reference material. This section assists you in adding new slides and moving around a collection of slides, which comprises a presentation.

Adding a new slide

Unless you are the most painfully concise human on the planet (kinda like the farmer in the movie *Babe*), I imagine you'll want more than a single slide in your PowerPoint presentation. You can add a new slide in any view, except Slide Show view. To add a new slide, you first need to open a presentation — either an existing presentation or a new one.

Add a new slide by using any of these procedures:

✦ Click the New Slide button on the Standard toolbar.

✦ Click the New Slide button in the Common Tasks toolbar.

✦ Choose Insert⇨New Slide from the menu bar.

Each time you add a new slide, you'll be presented with a New Slide dialog box.

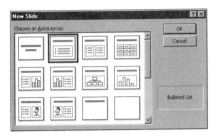

Using AutoLayout

The New Slide dialog box inquires how you want to format your newly created slide. Do you want a title slide, a slide with text bullets and clip art, or a slide with an organizational chart?

You can select from a whole bunch of (actually 21) slide layouts that PowerPoint automatically sets up for you. These design options are termed *AutoLayouts,* and they allow you to quickly and easily choose what you want your new slide to look like. An AutoLayout is not to be confused with that head-over-heels flipping maneuver that earned Nadia Comaneci a 10 at the 1976 Olympics.

Each new slide can be created using a different AutoLayout, allowing you to create a presentation with a variety of formats tailored to meet your specific needs.

Typing text on the slide

Each new slide you create reserves a partitioned zone where you can type your text (except for instances when you choose to create a completely blank slide). These "type here" zones are called *text boxes.* Notice that the placeholders Click to add title and Click to add text occupy the text boxes until you replace them with your own words.

Text boxes

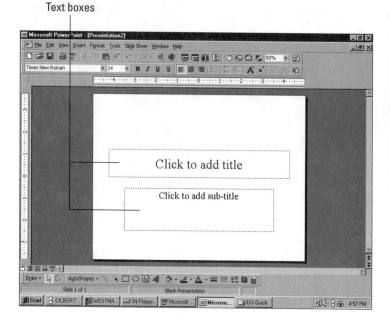

Keep the following in mind when you enter text:

✦ Typically you'll type a title in one text box (the title area), followed by a few text bullets in another text box located just below the title (the object area). You may even decide to delete text boxes or type on some other part of the slide altogether.

✦ Moving the cursor into a text box converts the cursor from an arrow to an I-beam, indicating that the text box is ready to accept text. When this happens, click the mouse anywhere in the box and start typing. Now PowerPoint acts like a word processor. The left and right arrow keys move you around, and the Delete key erases your typing.

✦ Words automatically wrap when they reach the right border of a text box, but if you want to move immediately to the next line press Enter. *See also* Part IV for more information about handling text.

Pasting a picture on the slide

The PowerPoint task you'll perform most often is typing text on a slide. The task you'll perform second most often is tracking down a relevant piece of clip art and pasting it on a slide. You may also choose to add photos, drawings, or scanned images to your slides — the possibilities are endless!

Following is the simplest way to add a picture:

1. Select an AutoLayout that includes a clip art placeholder.

2. Double-click the placeholder to access a catalog of clip art images.

3. Peruse and select a fitting image for your subject.

Upon exiting the art catalog, your chosen image will be magically glued to your slide. See Part V and VI for details on adding graphical images . . . or whenever the artistic spirit moves you.

Using a color scheme

Color schemes offer you the option of exercising your creative muscle to alter slide background colors, text colors, and accent colors. The schemes ensure that colors complement one another in an aesthetically pleasing combination, and that text readability is maximized relative to the background. Schemes offer light-on-dark combinations, dark-on-light combinations, bolds, brights, pastels, and neutrals.

Invoke color scheme options by choosing Format ➪ Slide Color Scheme from the menu bar. This action opens the Color Scheme dialog box.

The Color Scheme dialog box has two tabs, Standard and Custom. It also has a Preview button that you can press in order to examine how your Color Scheme choice will look before actually applying it to your slide or presentation. Here is what each tab does:

+ **Standard tab:** This tab offers a selection of premade Color schemes. Click the Color scheme you want for the current slide and press Apply. To apply the selected Color scheme to the entire presentation, press Apply to All.

+ **Custom tab:** This tab allows you to create your own color scheme. In the Scheme colors area, you can change the individual colors of the following items: Background, Text and lines, Shadows Title text, Fills, Accent, Accent and hyperlink, and Accent and followed hyperlink. To change an individual color, click the color then press Change Color and choose a new color at the Background Color dialog box that appears. After making your changes, press the Apply button to make the changes effective on the current slide only, or press the Apply to All button to make the changes effective on all slides in your presentation.

To save a scheme created within the Custom tab area of the Color Scheme dialog box, press A̲dd as Standard Scheme after making your individual color choices. Your new scheme will be added to the Standard tab of the Color Scheme dialog box.

Duplicating a slide

Duplicating a slide is an easy way to reuse the formatting of one slide as a guide for other slides. You will find duplicating particularly useful for churning out slides which have the same title and images with variations only on bullet items.

 You may also find duplicating a simple way to build a series of steps in a sequence: Just build the entire sequence on a slide, make a duplicate for each step, and delete the items on each slide that don't belong.

Duplicating is really just a one-step process for copying and pasting. To duplicate a slide, use the E̲dit⇨Dupl̲icate command, or press Ctrl+D. The currently selected slide is duplicated. If more than one slide is selected, every slide in the selection will be duplicated and placed immediately following the last selected slide.

Deleting a slide

Eliminating a slide can be accomplished in any view except during the Slide Show.

1. Select the slide to be deleted by clicking on it or moving to the slide in Slide View. To select multiple slide, move to Outline or Slide Sorter View, hold the shift key down and click on each slide to be deleted.

2. Delete your selection using the E̲dit⇨Cu̲t command. Alternatively, you may press the Backspace or Delete key to delete selected slides.

Moving between slides

You have several ways of moving from slide to slide during the construction of your PowerPoint presentation:

◆ Click an arrow on the scroll bar at the right side of the screen. The up arrow takes you toward your first slide. The down arrow takes you toward your last slide. The double arrows move you one slide at a time through your entire set of slides.

◆ Press PgUp or PgDn to move through your stack one slide at a time.

◆ Drag the right-side scroll box between the up and down arrows. As you drag, you'll see a small box indicating your current slide position in the stack.

Working in Outline View

In Outline view, your entire presentation appears as an outline comprised of the titles and body text from each slide. The benefit of working in Outline view is that it lets you organize and view text only, so that you can easily see how information progresses from slide to slide. You can construct your presentation focusing on text content without worrying about aesthetic appearance. Because the purpose of Outline view is to concentrate on the text of your slides, in this view you can only edit text content, text formatting, and text organization.

You can create a new presentation in Outline view, or you can switch to Outline view to peruse any existing PowerPoint presentation. You can move back and forth among Outline view and all other PowerPoint views at any time as you build and edit your presentations.

Brainstorming the content of new presentation is most easily accomplished in Outline view. You can quickly create slide after slide of key concepts by using Outline view as your construction mode — then later switch to Slide View to finesse the "look" of each slide.

Switch to outline view using either of these methods:

◆ Select View⇨Outline from the menu bar.

 ◆ Click the Outline view button, located in the bottom-left corner of the PowerPoint window.

How slides and text are organized

In Outline view, slides are listed vertically, from your first slide to your last. Each slide is designated by a number and a slide marker, which indicates whether the slide contains text-only or text and other media elements.

 You can quickly determine whether a slide contains text only or both text and other media by looking at its slide marker. The slide marker appears differently in each instance:

   ✦ **Text only slide:** Contains title and/or body text only. This marker is also used to represent a blank slide.

   ✦ **Text and other media slide:** Contains non-text elements of any type, such as drawing figures, clip art, sound files, or movies.

The slide title appears to the right of each slide marker, and body text, indented up to five levels, appears below the slide title. The body text may appear as paragraphs or bullet items, and can be easily moved — rearranged within a slide, or moved to other slides. Some repositioning tasks are accomplished by clicking and dragging the target text, and others are performed using buttons on the Outlining toolbar.

Outlining toolbar

Switching to Outline view summons an Outlining toolbar containing specialized buttons for working in Outline view. Outlining buttons deal primarily with repositioning text so that the text's significance is appropriately conveyed by its position relative to other text.

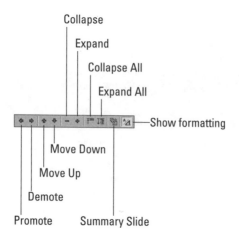

Buttons on the Outlining toolbar are

+ **Promote:** Elevates the position of the selected paragraph or bullet item by moving it up and left one heading level.

+ **Demote:** Diminishes the position of the selected paragraph or bullet item by moving it down and right one heading level.

+ **Move Up:** Repositions the selected paragraph or bullet item — and any collapsed subordinate text — up, above the preceding displayed paragraph or bullet item.

+ **Move Down:** Repositions the selected paragraph — and any collapsed subordinate text — down, below the following displayed paragraph.

+ **Collapse:** Hides body text to show only the title of the selected slide or slides. A slide with collapsed text has a thin gray line underlining its title.

+ **Expand:** Redisplays collapsed text of selected slides.

+ **Collapse All:** Collapses the body text of all slides in the presentation.

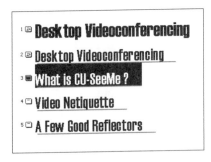

+ **Expand All:** Shows the body text of all slides in the presentation.

+ **Summary Slide:** Builds a new slide from the titles of selected slides. The title of the new slide is Summary Slide, and the titles of selected slides appear as bullets. The summary slide is inserted in front of the first selected slide (serving more as an agenda slide, than a summary slide).

✦ **Show Formatting:** Toggles on/off to show or hide text format-ting (such as font and point size) in Outline view.

Building a new presentation

To create a new presentation in Outline view:

1. Choose File⇨New from the menu bar, and select a presenta-tion type from the New Presentation dialog box.

2. Select View⇨Outline from the menu bar, or press the Outline view button.

3. Choose an AutoLayout from the New Slide dialog box.

An empty slide marker for Slide 1 appears in Outline view.

4. Type a title for Slide 1, and press Enter.

5. Click the Demote button on the Outlining toolbar, or press Enter and Tab to create the first bullet level.

Type text for the first bullet and press Enter. Continue typing and pressing Enter to create as many bullet items as you want.

6. After the final bullet item, press Ctrl+Enter or press Enter and the Promote button on the Outlining toolbar to create the next slide.

7. Repeat Step 4 through Step 6 to create as many slides as you want.

8. Choose File⇨Save from the menu bar, or press the Save button on the Standard toolbar.

Name your presentation and press Save.

You can press a different view button at any time to examine how your presentation looks in other views.

Changing the position of a title or paragraph

Change the position of a slide title or paragraph as follows:

1. In Outline view, select the title or paragraph you wish to move.

2. Drag the selected text to a new position, or click Promote, Demote, Move Up, or Move Down to reposition the selected text.

Changing slide order in an outline

Move an entire slide to a different position in the outline as follows:

1. In Outline view, click and hold the slide marker representing the slide you want to move. The pointer will change to a compass when it moves over the slide marker.

The text of the entire slide — title and body text — will be selected.

2. Drag the selected slide to a new position, or click Move Up or Move Down to reposition the selected text.

The entire presentation of slides will reorder to reflect the repositioning of the moved slide.

Viewing a slide thumbnail

While working in Outline view, you can obtain a quick view of how the current slide looks — without switching to Slide view. To open a window showing a thumbnail version of the current slide, right-click the mouse and select Slide Miniature from the menu. Clicking the slide thumbnail will display the transition applied to the current slide.

Opening a Saved Presentation

Once you've constructed and saved a file of slides, you'll need to open it back up (at some later time) for display during your presentation. You may also wish to reopen the file for further editing, or to add some additional slides.

Retrieve your previously created presentation one of these ways:

+ Click the Open button on the Standard toolbar.

+ Use the File⇨Open command.

+ Press Ctrl+O or Ctrl+F12.

Each method summons the Open dialog box revealing lots of files from which you should hunt down and reclaim the one you require. When you find the file you want, double-click it, or click it once and press OK.

Printing Slides and Handouts

Ah, Gutenberg would be proud if he were aware of the ease and beauty with which we print documents nowadays. (That's Johannes Gutenberg, not Steve Gutenberg.) Summon the Print dialog box by choosing File⇨Print.

PowerPoint offers some fabulous print options under the Print what tab:

✦ **Slides:** This is your transparency-making option. It prints your slides full page with one slide per page. Slides can be printed with or without animations. If you choose to print with animations, each printed page will contain one additional animation until all animations are completed for a slide.

✦ **Handouts — two, three, or six per page:** Handouts are great for filling in meeting no-shows.

✦ **Notes Pages:** Your lecture "kit" complete with a visual of each slide accompanied by every comment you plan to make about the slide.

✦ **Outline View:** Provides you a short text-only summary of what information is on which slide as you deliver your presentation to the class.

After you decide what you want to print, turn on your printer, load it with paper — or transparencies — and print using one of these methods:

✦ Click the Print button on the Standard toolbar

✦ Use File⇨Print

✦ Press Ctrl+P or Ctrl+Shift+F12

Printing is covered in depth in Part IX.

Showing a Presentation

After creating a PowerPoint masterpiece, you'll want to deliver your presentation to your intended audience. Your presentation, or slide show, can be shown as overhead transparencies, 35mm slides, computer display, or on the World Wide Web.

Computer display is by far the most common method for showing PowerPoint presentations:

✦ Running a slide show via computer offers the capability to run attention-capturing sounds, movies, and animations.

✦ It's also the most time-saving and resource-efficient presentation method, because it requires no physical product to be created.

To run a PowerPoint slide show, move to the first slide in your presentation and then press the Slide Show View button in the lower-left corner of the screen. Alternatively, you may start the show by selecting Slide Show⇨View Show from the menu bar. Each slide will fill the screen completely.

✦ To advance the slides, click the mouse button or press the forward arrow on the keyboard.

✦ Click the backward arrow to display the previous slide.

✦ Pressing Esc exits the Slide Show mode.

Showing a PowerPoint presentation is covered in depth in Part VIII.

Part III

Laying the Groundwork: Working with Templates and Masters

Unless you're particularly fond of the minimalist school of artistic design, you want to create slides featuring more than just black text on white backgrounds. You want backgrounds with color, shading, highlights (and maybe a little off the top . . . oops, this isn't a haircut). This part gives you the lowdown on building beautiful backgrounds by using templates.

The next step after choosing a template is to adjust the colors, graphics, and text styles to suit your needs by editing the Slide Master, Title Master, Handout Master, and Notes Master. The Masters are particularly useful entities because they provide you a quick and easy way to set up slide attributes for your entire presentation. Unless you specifically choose to override the Master on a given slide, all slides follow the design specifications you establish on the Masters.

In this part . . .

- ✔ Shopping for a template
- ✔ Creating your own template
- ✔ Setting up Master formats
- ✔ Using headers and footers
- ✔ Modifying slide backgrounds
- ✔ Setting up the title slide
- ✔ Making adjustments to individual slides

About Templates and Masters

The fastest, most effective way to put together an attractive, professional-looking PowerPoint presentation is to take advantage of templates and customize them to suit your needs:

1. Use a template to start creating your presentation right away. The PowerPoint templates provide preformatted, professionally designed backgrounds, images, and text colors that make for readable, eye-catching slides. (Some of the templates also provide content that you may want to use.)

2. Make adjustments to the template — formatting changes or the addition of *theme elements* (text and objects that will appear on every slide) — for all your slides at one time by editing the Slide Master. As you construct each slide, you can override the Master and make necessary changes to each slide individually.

3. Modify the Title Master to make your title slide (the first slide of the presentation) stand out from the rest of the presentation.

4. Use the Handout Master to layout how your presentation will appear as a hard copy audience handout.

5. Use the Notes Master to organize how your speaker notes will appear in hard copy form.

See the rest of this part for details on these steps.

Applying and Creating Templates

PowerPoint comes stocked with tons of premade *templates* — artistic blueprints for constructing your slide presentations quickly and easily. Templates are set up with predefined formatting settings to minimize the time and effort you expend in building slides; you can then adjust the template however you want for an individual presentation by modifying the Slide Master. If you find that you keep making the same adjustments over and over again, you can also create your own template.

Applying a template to a new or an existing presentation

You can apply a template to a new presentation, as you start up PowerPoint, or you can change the template midway through working on a presentation:

✦ **New presentation:** Click the <u>T</u>emplate option in the start-up dialog box that appears when you first start PowerPoint.

✦ **Existing presentation:** Open the presentation and either choose Format➪Apply Design or double-click the name of the template in the status bar at the bottom of the PowerPoint window.

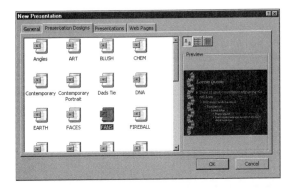

 If you apply a new template midway through the construction of your PowerPoint presentation, be aware that the template is applied to all slides in the entire presentation. PowerPoint does not allow a mix-and-match approach: You cannot use one template for a few slides and another template for a few others.

 Also be aware that applying a new template obliterates any modifications that you made to the Slide Master for the previously used template. Applying a new template copies the template's background colors, text formatting, decorations — everything — onto your Masters and all slides throughout the presentation.

Changes made to the colors and formatting of non-Master items on individual slides, though, aren't impacted by the application of the new template. Any custom-tailoring of non-Master elements on individual slides (except background color) remains safe, as PowerPoint preserves such deviations regardless of changes in the Master.

Whether you're applying the template to a new or an existing presentation, here's what you do next:

1. In the dialog box that appears, choose a template from one of these locations:

• **Presentations folder:** Contains 38 content-formatted templates, such as Corporate Financial Overview, using around 15 different styles. You'll probably want to dump the content and just use the template styles. Project Status and Personal Home Page (which is great for you World Wide Web junkies) are two of my favorites.

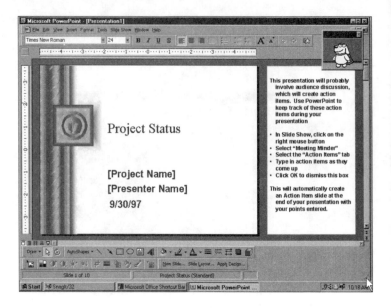

- **Presentation Designs folder:** Contains around 17 ready-to-go templates without content. The styles differ from those in the Presentation folder, and the designs are just gorgeous. Check out Portrait Notebook and Angles.

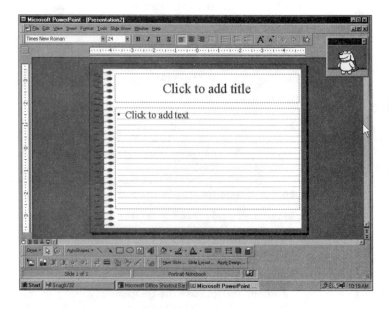

- **Web Pages folder:** Contains two templates to assist you in creating presentations intended for display on the web.

- **Microsoft PowerPoint CD:** In case the templates in those three folders aren't enough, you can find 41 bonus Windows templates in the CD from which you installed PowerPoint on your computer. Just look on the CD in the folder Valupack\Templates\Design for additional templates.

2. Click a template once to check out a thumbnail sketch of it. Then click OK to apply the template.

3. If you are creating a new presentation, PowerPoint now asks you to choose a layout for your first slide. Go ahead and click a layout. Now, you probably want to tweak the template a bit to suit your own purposes and preferences; *See* "Editing the Slide Master" in this part for details on how to do that.

4. If you are updating an existing presentation, you will now see the new template applied to your slides. If you want to tweak the template, see "Editing the Slide Master" in this part for further details.

Creating an original template

Don't like any of PowerPoint's templates? Create your own! A template is basically just a PowerPoint presentation with no slides, so creating your own is easy:

1. Choose File⇨New.

2. Click Cancel in the Add New Slide dialog box.

3. Modify the template by choosing View⇨Masters. (*See also* "Editing the Slide Master" in this part.)

4. Save your newly created template by choosing File⇨Save.

Store your new template in the same folder as the other PowerPoint templates so you know where to look when trying to retrieve it. Your PowerPoint templates are probably stored in Program Files⇨Microsoft Office⇨Templates. Choose a subfolder within Templates, or create a new one for your own special creations.

The typical PowerPoint template extension is POT. If you create a new template titled, "Wacky," save it in the templates folder by the name, Wacky.POT. Under Save as Type, select Presentation Template.

The next time you peruse template choices within PowerPoint, you'll see your newly created template appear among the template options.

Editing the Handout Master

The Handout Master allows you to lay out your presentation as it will appear as a hard copy audience handout. Put simply, it's a blueprint that defines whether handouts will show the presentation outline or small versions of the presentation slides. If you choose to show small versions of the presentation slides, the Handout Master also allows you to choose how many slide images will appear on the printed page. You have the option of two slides per page, three slides per page, or six slides per page.

You also have the option of adding placeholders on the Handout Master for the date, page number, header and footer. Headers are placed at the top of the handouts, and footers are placed at the bottom. After adding any placeholder, you can click on it to update the font and format of the text contained within that placeholder. If you add date or page number placeholders to the Handout Master, these fields will be automatically updated. For header and footer placeholders, clicking inside each placeholder allows you to insert text or edit text previously typed there.

Here's how you format the Handout Master for your presentation:

1. From any view, Choose View⇨Master⇨Handout Master.

This summons the Handout Master to appear.

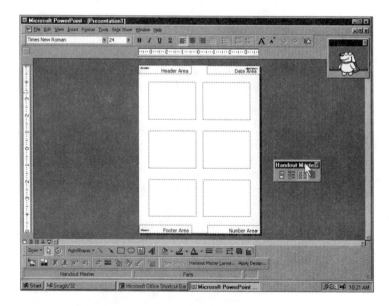

2. Right-click the mouse to open the Handout Master Layout dialog box.

3. At the Handout Master Layout dialog box, click the selection box of all placeholders you want located on the Master.

Placeholders already in use will be deselected.

4. At the Handout Master toolbox, click whether you want two slides per page, three per page, six per page, or the presentation outline shown on the handouts.

The Handout Master generates dashed outlines showing where the slides or outline will be printed. If you inadvertently close the Handout Master toolbar or it does not otherwise appear onscreen, you can cause it to rematerialize by choosing View⇨Toolbars⇨Handout Master.

When you are finished formatting the Handout Master, click on any view button to return to working on your presentation. Alternatively, you may choose to print and peruse your handouts by choosing File⇨Print.

Editing the Notes Master

The Notes Master dictates how your presentation's speaker notes will appear in hard copy form. It serves as a handy guide for laying out the position and relative size of the slide thumbnail, speaker note text, and other information you may want included on your notes.

The Notes Master gives you the option of adding placeholders. You can add placeholders for

+ **Slide image:** Must be resized by clicking either placeholder and adjusting its sizing handles

+ **Body:** Must be resized by clicking on either placeholder and adjusting its sizing handles

+ **Date**

+ **Header:** Reserves a small zone for placing text at the top of each notes page

+ **Footer:** Reserves a zone for placing text at the bottom of each notes page

After adding any placeholder, you can click on the placeholder and drag it to anywhere on the Notes Master page to reposition it. You can also click on any placeholder and edit the font and format of the text contained within that placeholder. If you choose to add date or page number placeholders to the Notes Master, these fields will be automatically updated. For body, header, and footer placeholders, clicking inside each placeholder allows you to insert text or edit text previously typed there. Any text you type inside these placeholders on the Notes Master will appear on all notes pages printouts you generate.

Here's how you format the Notes Master for your presentation:

1. From any view, Choose <u>V</u>iew⇨<u>M</u>aster⇨<u>N</u>otes Master. This calls up the Notes Master.

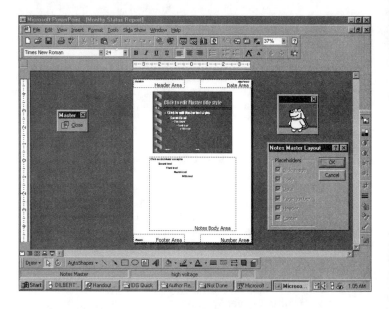

2. Right-click the mouse to open the Notes Master <u>L</u>ayout dialog box.

3. At the Notes Master Layout dialog box, click the selection box of all placeholders you want located on the Master.

Placeholders already in use will be deselected.

On the Notes Master layout, click once on the slide miniature and resize it to make adequate room for the body placeholder.

4. On the Notes Master layout, click once on the body place-holder and resize it to ensure you have sufficient room for adding notes for each slide in your presentation.

When you finish formatting the Notes Master, click on any view button to return to working on your presentation. See Part VIII for information on adding speaker notes to individual slides.

Editing the Slide Master

After applying a template, you can make adjustments to it by fiddling with your presentation's Slide Master, which controls all aspects of how slides are constructed: background color; font, size, and color of the text; and display of any decorations, borders, or logos.

Every slide in your presentation uses the Slide Master format as a blueprint (unless you specify otherwise). Changing the Master impacts every slide in the presentation — adding a polka-dot border to the Master adds a polka-dot border to each and every one of your slides.

  If you build a fabulous 20-slide presentation and then change your Slide Master in some bizarre, disfiguring way, every single one of your previously fabulous slides reflects that change.

Here's how to modify the Slide Master:

1. Choose View➪Master➪Slide Master or Shift+click the Slide view button to bring up the Slide Master.

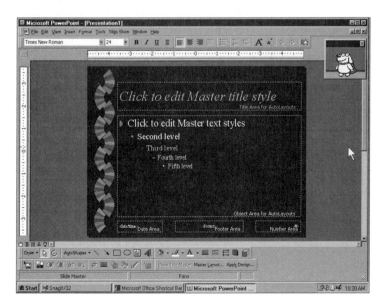

Notice that a solid or shaded color typically fills the background, and one or more objects (such as drawn shapes or clip art images) adorn the otherwise plain color. Additionally, you see placeholders for the slide title and body text.

The Slide Master also includes placeholders for the objects that appear at the bottom of each slide: the Date Area, Footer Area, and Number Area. (*See also* "Inserting headers and footers" later in this section.)

2. Edit the Slide Master as you want. (*See also* Part IV for details about formatting text, and Part V for information on editing graphical elements.)

PowerPoint applies text format changes to entire paragraphs in the Master — just click anywhere within the paragraph, and your formatting changes apply to the whole schmear.

The Master text styles in the body object have five different levels. You can change how the text and bullets are formatted on each level independently of every other level.

Incidentally, if you type specific text in the Title or Object Area placeholders, it doesn't appear on the slides. Placeholder text is shown only as an example of the style and placement of text on your slides. You can create text items that recur on all slides, but not by using the Title or Object Area text boxes. In fact, you must be certain to stay out of the official text boxes when creating theme text; *See* "Adding theme elements" later in this section.

If the text boxes on your Slide Master are bumping into other Master items (such as clip art) just click the text box and reposition it by dragging it to a new location. Resizing a text box can be accomplished by selecting the text box (with a single click) then adjusting one of the *handles* which mark the edges of the box.

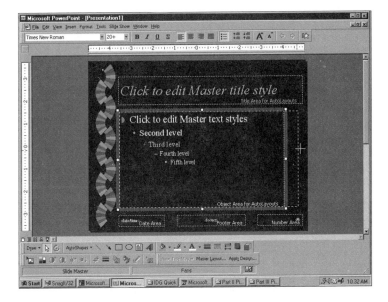

To adjust a handle, click on it and drag it to a new location. You'll know you can select a handle when your regular cursor arrow converts to a small double-tipped arrow. After selecting a handle, you'll notice that the double-tipped arrow converts to a small cross and stays that way as you resize the box.

To maintain the proportions of a text box, hold the shift key down during resizing. By the way, resizing via the object handles applies not just to text boxes, but to all other objects you'll add to the Master.

3. Choose View⇨Slide, or click the Slide view button, or click the X in the upper-right corner of the floating Master toolbar (or toolbox, considering its diminutive size) to close the Slide Master.

Voilà! Your slides magically metamorphose as per the changes made on the Slide Master.

Adding theme elements

Anything that you can put on an individual slide can be put on the Slide Master, to appear on every slide in the presentation. For example, you may want to put the name of the presentation or a sound on the Master. Here's how you add theme text or objects to the Master so that the element appears on every slide:

1. Choose View⇔Master⇔Slide Master or Shift+click the Slide view button.

2. To add theme text, click the Text Tool button on the Drawing toolbar. The mouse cursor turns into a pogo stick whenever you're outside the Title and Object Area text boxes. So stay outside the text boxes! You can add other theme objects, like images or video, anywhere on the Master.

3. For theme text, click the location — anywhere except in the Title Area or the Object Area — where you want to add the text. PowerPoint creates a text box (a small box with the blinking vertical line) wherever you click. You do not need to specify where theme objects should be placed — once they are added to the Master you can reposition objects anywhere you want them.

4. Type your theme text or insert your theme object. *See* Part III and Part IV for details about text and multimedia objects, respectively.

5. Format the text or object. For theme text, you may want to choose a really funky font — one you wouldn't typically use for main text on the slides because of readability issues. Funky is fine for theme text. Other objects like clip art can be formatted (recolored, resized, and so on) to suit your taste as well.

6. Click the Slide view button to see your theme text and objects appear on all your slides. If you don't like how they look, go back to the Master and modify your work.

Inserting headers and footers

PowerPoint 97 gives you an easy method of applying several finishing touches to your presentation in the footer of each slide. It also allows you to add both headers and footers to notes and handout pages. Footers are automatically placed at the bottom of a PowerPoint slide or page, and headers are placed at the top. Regardless of their initial positions, however, you can reposition their placement to best suit your needs. Here's how to insert headers and footers:

1. Choose <u>V</u>iew⇨<u>H</u>eader and Footer to bring up the Header and
Footer dialog box.

2. Fill in any of the following boxes:

- **Date Area:** Displays the date and time

- **Number Area:** Displays the slide number

- **Footer Area:** Displays any other recurring text that you want
  to place on your slides

You can reposition the three areas anywhere on the slides by
switching to the Slide or Title Master and then dragging the
placeholders to new locations.

Avoid typing in placeholder markers such as the `<date,time>`.
The computer updates these markers according to its internal
clock, so that PowerPoint displays the actual date and time at
which you give your presentation. Delete these markers if you
intend to place some other date or time on your Master.

You can also edit the header and footer placeholders directly by
displaying the Master, clicking on each placeholder, and typing in
your information.

Choosing colors for backgrounds

PowerPoint offers incredibly flexible options for tinting your
slides. You can fuss with minute details of coloring the Slide
Master, but letting PowerPoint serve as your personal designer is a
whole lot easier. Here's how to use one of the well-coordinated,
visually appealing color schemes that PowerPoint offers you (and
how to adjust the colors to your liking, if you're the persnickety
type):

1. Choose <u>V</u>iew⇨<u>M</u>aster⇨<u>S</u>lide Master or Shift+click the Slide
view button.

2. Choose Format⇨Slide Color to bring up the Color Scheme dialog box.

3. Choose an option:

To pick a PowerPoint color scheme: Click the Standard tab and double-click a scheme you like to accept it.

To change the colors of individual scheme elements: Click the Custom tab, double-click any element in the Color Scheme dialog box, and choose a new color.

You can also change the shading of the background slide color to obtain a richer feel than just plain old brown or plain old orange. To alter background shading:

1. Choose Format⇨Background to open the Background dialog box.

2. Click the color drop-down menu and click Fill Effects. This opens the Fill Effects dialog box.

3. Click the Gradient tab and click one or two colors, along with a Shading style. The Shading style allows you to select how the selected colors will be blended together on the slide backgrounds: horizontally, vertically, or some other combination.

The Fill Effects dialog box also has Texture, Pattern, and Picture tabs.

- **Texture:** I definitely recommend trying out several of the textures as backgrounds — some of them are absolutely beautiful!

- **Pattern:** Stay away from using patterns; they make text extremely hard to read.

- **Picture:** Be cautious about using imported pictures, which can also create readability problems. Use background pictures only when they don't compete with text that will appear on top of them.

As you tinker with assorted selections, click the Preview button at any time to test out your chosen backgrounds.

Keep these tips in mind:

✦ Steer clear of red and avoid busy patterns (checkerboard, thin stripes, Scottish plaid, and so on). These "extremes" tend not to display well, especially when routing slide presentations via the computer.

✦ Midnight blue, dark green, and purple make beautiful backgrounds, particularly when paired with white or yellow text.

✦ Shaded backgrounds look great when blending colors of similar intensities. For example, black and the darkest shade of magenta blend well; beige and pastel yellow blend well, too.

✦ Use white as the primary background color when making transparencies.

✦ Use any color *except* white as the primary background color when making on-screen and 35mm slides.

Deleting Master components

Deleting an object on the Slide Master is a snap:

1. Retrieve the Slide Master by Shift+clicking the Slide view button or choosing View➪Master➪Slide Master.

2. Click the object that you want to delete. To wipe out an entire text object, first click anywhere on the text and then click again on the object frame.

3. Press the Backspace or Delete key or choose Edit➪Cut.

If you erroneously delete an object, just undo your mistake by choosing Edit➪Undo from the menu bar.

Note: You can't move or edit Slide Master elements from the slides themselves. I've wasted plenty of time trying to delete a theme picture on Slide #7 only to realize (after much frustration) that I can't grab the darn thing because it's not on the slide — it's on the Master.

Editing the Title Master

PowerPoint 97 offers you a separate Title Master for designing title slides. The idea is that you can use it to lay out your title slide differently than the rest of your slide presentation. I usually don't take the time to fidget with the Title Master, but you're welcome to have at it.

Call up the Title Master as follows:

1. In Slide view, move to the first slide in your slide presentation by sliding the right-hand scroll bar all the way to the top. (This assumes that the first slide is the title slide.)

2. Choose View➪Master➪Title Master.

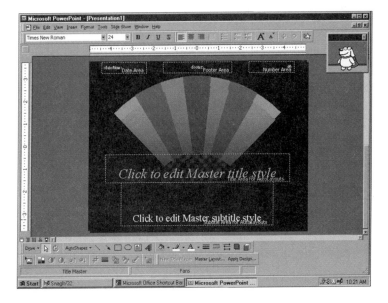

3. Alter the Title Master to your heart's content. See "Editing the Slide Master" for additional details.

The Title Master differs from — but coordinates nicely with — the Slide Master for a given template. Note, however, that the Object Area for AutoLayouts is replaced with Subtitle Area for AutoLayouts. The only difference this makes is that less room is reserved in the lower half of the Title Slide for placing text. Remember, though, that you can always resize — or even delete — a text box to meet your own specific requirements.

Overriding the Master Style on a Single Slide

Using Masters is optional, but just as you wouldn't build a house without a floor plan, you wouldn't want to build a PowerPoint presentation without Masters. Why waste time performing the same ten formatting steps on each of 20 slides when you can format them once on the Master and be done with it?

You can, however, disregard the Master format for a particular slide, which allows you to modify individual slides as needed without impacting the rest of your presentation. The processes of adding and moving text and objects on an individual slide are the same as for the Master slides.

Changing the text formatting

Suppose you've spent nine slides leading up to a critical, culminating key point, and to ensure that every participant's brain captures and processes this super-important key point, you want to use bright gold, italic, 60-point Impact — but just on this one slide.

Here's how you make changes to the Master style on one particular slide:

1. Move to the slide where you want to make the change.

2. Switch to Slide view.

 3. Click the Text Tool button and select (highlight) the text that you want to edit. Use the Text Formatting toolbar to make your changes. The changes don't impact the Slide Master; they apply to this individual slide only.

Changing the background color

If you want to change the background color on a single slide, just follow these steps:

1. In any view, move to the slide where you want to use a different background.

2. Choose Format⇨Background to bring up the Background dialog box.

3. Click the color tab to reveal the drop-down menu for changing the background color to your preference. *See* "Choosing colors for objects and backgrounds" in this part.

4. Click the Apply button to make the changes take effect on the current slide.

 Do *not* click the Apply to all button, or every slide in your presentation will be affected.

Clicking the Apply to all button at this stage is a convenient way of editing the Slide Master without opening up the Master itself.

Deleting background objects

To obliterate the Master objects from a given slide, follow these steps:

1. In Slide view, move to the slide where you want to delete background objects.

2. Choose Format⇨Background to bring up the Background dialog box.

3. Click the Omit background graphics from master check box so that a check mark appears in the box.

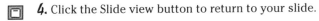 *4.* Click the Slide view button to return to your slide.

Reverting to the Master style

If you don't like the changes you've made to the individual slide, you can choose Edit⇨Undo to undo your most recent change. Or if you want to return the entire slide back to the Slide Master style, here's what you do:

1. Switch to Slide view by choosing View⇨Slide or clicking the Slide view button.

2. Choose Format⇨Slide Layout to bring up the Slide Layout dialog box.

3. Click the Reapply button to restore all formatting to that specified by the Slide Master.

Part IV

Adding Text

The single most important element you place on your slides is text. After all, the text is what conveys the essence of your presentation — the key points that you want your audience to remember. This part shows you how to present that text in the most effective way.

The material discussed in this part applies to all PowerPoint text. Procedures for formatting text on the Masters are identical for formatting text on individual slides. The fastest way to format text for an entire presentation is to format text in the text boxes located on the Slide and Title Masters. Text on all slides in the presentation will follow this formatting, eliminating the need for you to format text on a slide-by-slide basis. Individual text boxes on any slide can be reformatted as needed, overriding the formatting prescribed for them by the Masters.

In this part . . .

- ✔ Working with text boxes
- ✔ Aligning blocks of text
- ✔ Aligning text with indents and tabs
- ✔ Adding bullets
- ✔ Quickly changing capitalization
- ✔ Cutting, copying, and pasting text
- ✔ Finding and replacing text
- ✔ Modifying the appearance of your text
- ✔ Checking your spelling
- ✔ Undoing errors

About Text Boxes

All slides — the Slide Master, the Title Master, and all slide AutoLayouts except the Blank slide option — appear with at least one text box (a zone specially reserved for adding text).

Here's what you should know about text boxes:

+ You can enlarge or shrink a text box, but you can't change its shape — text boxes are always rectangular.

+ Text boxes are marked by lightly dashed lines. You type inside the boundaries of each box, although your typed text may or may not actually fill up the entire box.

+ You can move text boxes around on the slide, which is useful when a text box bumps into another slide element, such as clip art.

+ You can delete text boxes and add new ones, as needed.

Adding text boxes

You can add as many text boxes to a slide as you like. Each text box can be formatted and moved independently from all other text boxes. To add a text box:

1. Click the Text box button on the Drawing toolbar.

2. Point the I-beam cursor to position the upper-left hand corner of your new text box.

3. Click and hold the mouse while dragging to position the lower right-hand corner of your new text box.

The cursor will appear as a crosshair during the positioning, and you see solid edges appear as the borders of the box.

4. Release the mouse button when the text box obtains the desired proportions.

The new text box is now complete. Click inside the box to type text, or click the edge of the box to format how text appears inside the box.

Selecting text boxes

Before you can modify a text box, you have to identify for PowerPoint which text box you want to work on. To select a text box:

1. Click the Select Objects button, also known as the pointer, on the Drawing toolbar.

2. Point the pointer anywhere along the border of the text box that you want to edit; then click the left mouse button.

The text box suddenly sprouts *handles* — dots marking the corners and sides of the box. The appearance of handles indicates that the text box is selected.

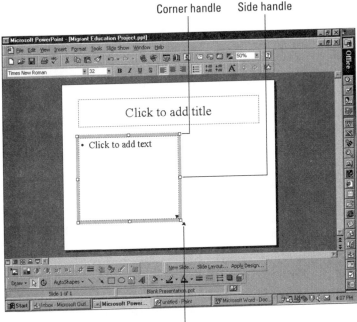

Corner handle   Side handle

Resizing text box

Resizing or moving text boxes

After you select a text box, you're free to resize and move the box as you want. Go wild! And follow these simple guidelines along the way:

✦ **To move a text box:** Click and hold down the mouse button anywhere along the edge of the text box — except on a handle! Then drag the box anywhere on the slide and release.

✦ **To change the size of a text box while keeping the original proportions:** Click and hold down the mouse button on any of the corner handles, drag the handle to enlarge or shrink the text box proportionally, and then release. To keep the box centered, hold down the Ctrl key while resizing.

✦ **To change the proportions of a text box:** Click and hold down the mouse button on any of the side handles. Drag the top or bottom handle to increase or shrink the text box's height; drag the left or right handle to adjust the width.

Importing text from a word processing program into a text box

You may import text from outside PowerPoint (such as from a word processing program) for inclusion in a text box. Import text as follows:

1. In your word processing program, select the text you wish to copy onto the PowerPoint slide.

2. In your word processing program, copy the selected text by pressing Edit⇨Copy or Ctrl +C.

3. In PowerPoint, click on the slide to which the copied text will be added.

4. In PowerPoint, click inside the text box where you wish to add the copied text.

5. In PowerPoint, paste the selected text by pressing Edit⇨Paste or Ctrl + V.

Moving around and typing inside a text box

You type and edit text in a PowerPoint text box in virtually the same way that you use a word processor. But first you have to tell PowerPoint that you want to manipulate the text:

1. Click the Select Objects button (pointer) on the Drawing toolbar.

2. Move the pointer into the text box. A thick border appears around the text box, a solid background color appears behind the text, and the pointer changes to an I-beam once inside the text box — all of which indicate that you can now start typing.

Here are some things to know about typing and editing in a text box:

✦ **Wrapping words to the next line:** When you reach the end of a line, keep typing — PowerPoint automatically moves to the next line. You press Enter only when you want to begin a new paragraph.

✦ **Using the keyboard to navigate through the text:** Use the ↑, ↓, ←, and → keys on your keyboard to move the cursor up or down one line, or left or right by one character.

✦ **Using the mouse to navigate through the text:** Move the mouse until the little I-beam is positioned where you want to make an edit, and then click the left mouse button. The I-beam cursor instantly repositions itself to your chosen destination.

✦ **Selecting text (marking text to be edited):** Use one of these methods:

- Press the Shift key while simultaneously pressing an arrow key to highlight an entire block of text.

- Use the mouse to point to the beginning of the text that you want to mark; then click and drag the mouse over the text. The affected text is highlighted as you drag. Release the button when you reach the end of the block.

✦ **Deleting text:** Press the Backspace key or the Delete key to delete highlighted (selected) text. To delete one character to the left of the cursor, press Backspace; to delete one character to the right of the cursor, press Delete.

If you change text attributes (formatting, aligning, and so on) without first marking a block of text, the changes kick in at the cursor location. In other words, you see your selected text change as soon as you start typing. Repositioning the cursor to another location, however, does not carry with it the text formatting you've established.

Aligning Paragraphs of Text

Adjust the way your text lines up by selecting an entire text box or selecting only specific lines of text within a text box. Then choose Format⇨Alignment or click the appropriate toolbar button to align your selected text. PowerPoint provides you with all the familiar ways to align text on your slides:

✦ **Centered:** Most of the time, you want to center the title of each slide — it looks most visually appealing that way. Multiple slides on the same topic can have the title centered on the first slide and deleted altogether on all subsequent, related slides. Short, unbulleted text items also look nice centered, as differences in the length of each line help effectively distinguish line items.

 ✦ **Left-aligned:** For bulleted body text, use left alignment.

 ✦ **Right-aligned:** Right alignment is appropriate when creating a list of pairs and you want the second items in the pairs to line up neatly down the right-hand side of the text box.

 ✦ **Justified:** Justified alignment is useful when presenting an entire paragraph of unbulleted narrative on your PowerPoint slide.

Aligning Text with Indents and Tabs

Each individual text box has its own ruler for measuring the length of the box and for setting the location of indents and tabs within the box. Settings you define for this ruler affect all text within the box. You can establish different settings for different text boxes, but not for individual lines of text within a box.

To align text by setting indents and tabs:

1. Turn on the ruler by selecting <u>V</u>iew⇨<u>R</u>uler.

2. Click inside the text box in which you wish to set indents and tabs.

3. Click and drag the upper margin setting to define the indent position for new paragraphs within the text box.

4. Click and drag the lower margin setting to define the indent position for paragraph bodies within the text box.

5. Click the tab button to select a tab type, and then click a ruler position to add the tab to the ruler.

Bulleting Text

A bullet marks the start of a line to indicate a new text item. Bullets come in many styles, including spots, check marks, and arrows — but they're almost never shaped like real-life bullets.

Follow these steps to bullet your text in PowerPoint:

1. Select (highlight) the items or paragraphs that you want to bullet.

 2. Click the Bullet button.

The Bullet button operates like an on/off switch (a toggle). Following these steps adds bullets to unbulleted text; repeating the steps removes the bullets.

If you don't like the style of the bullets that appear on-screen, choose F<u>o</u>rmat⇨<u>B</u>ullet to call up the Bullet dialog box, where you can adjust the font, size, color, and character of different bullets until you find one you're happy with. Make sure that the Use a bullet check box is checked if you do indeed want the bullet to appear on-screen.

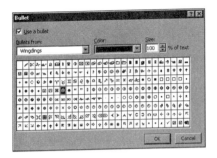

I recommend setting bullet attributes on the Slide Master in order to save time constructing your individual slides. *See* Part III.

Changing Capitalization for Blocks of Text

To quickly change the capitalization of text — a single character or a block of text — follow these steps:

1. Select the text that you want to capitalize.

2. Choose Format⇨Change Case, or Shift+F3.

3. Click a capitalization option from the Change Case menu and click OK.

- **Sentence case:** The first letter of the first word in each sentence is capitalized. All other text is changed to lowercase.

- **lowercase:** All text is changed to lowercase.

- **UPPERCASE:** All text is changed to uppercase.

- **Title Case:** The first letter of each word is capitalized except for articles, such as *a* and *the*.

- **tOGGLE cASE:** Uppercase letters are changed to lowercase and vice versa. I've never used this feature. Let me know if you find a reason for it.

Cutting, Copying, and Pasting Text

PowerPoint uses the same standard Cut, Copy, and Paste commands that are forever present in all Windows-based programs. All three editing commands operate on currently selected text, using the Clipboard as a holding buffer for the text (or other object) most recently cut or copied.

Button	Command	Keystroke	Menu
✂	Cut	Ctrl+X	Edit⇨Cut
📋	Copy	Ctrl+C	Edit⇨Copy
📋	Paste	Ctrl+V	Edit⇨Paste

Some thoughts to bear in mind when working with Cut, Copy, and Paste:

✦ **Duplicate text:** Select the text that you want to copy; then copy it. Click the cursor wherever you want to paste; then paste. The text appears in both locations. You can paste on the same slide or on any other slide in your presentation.

✦ **Duplicate an entire text box:** Choose Edit⇨Duplicate. This command works only when the text box itself is selected. Duplicate is disabled when text within a text box is selected. To duplicate selected text within a text box, use Copy and Paste.

✦ **Move text:** Select the text that you want cut; then cut it. Click the cursor wherever you want the text to reappear; then paste. The text appears only in the pasted location. You can paste on the same slide or on any other slide in your presentation.

✦ **Delete text:** Use the Cut command, which lets you get your text back if you suddenly change your mind (just press Paste). If you're absolutely certain that you want to eradicate certain text forever, select it and choose Edit⇨Clear. The Paste command can't bring back cleared text — that text is gone forever unless you immediately invoke the Undo command.

Finding and Replacing Text

The Find and Replace commands are helpful when you need to change one piece of text that appears several times throughout your slides — for example, the date on a series of slides that you want to reuse from a long-ago presentation.

The Find command locates specific words or phrases in your slide stack. Here's how to use it:

1. Choose Edit⇨Find to bring up the Find dialog box.

A Find dialog box appears. And PowerPup (if you've chosen PowerPup as your assistant) dons his Superdog cape and flies through the air to begin searching for your lost text, or a bone, whatever comes first.

2. Type in the Find what box the text that you want to locate. If you want to obtain an exact match of capital and lowercase letters, click the Match case box.

3. Press Enter to initiate the search.

   If your chosen text is located anywhere among your slides, the Find command moves to the first slide containing that text. It also highlights your found text so you can then edit it or continue searching for the next occurrence.

   If you choose to replace your found text with something else, click the Replace button or press Ctrl+H and type away.

   If you receive a message that the search item wasn't found, that means your search term wasn't located among your slides. Check your spelling and try again.

4. When you're done finding text, click Close in the Find dialog box, or press Enter to close the box.

If you already know you'll be replacing all instances of a given word — like substituting this year's date for the one from two years ago — invoke the Replace command instead of Find:

1. Choose Edit⇨Replace to call up the Replace dialog box.

2. In the Find what box, type the word or phrase that you want to replace.

3. In the Replace with box, type your replacement text.

4. Click the Replace All button. Every instance of the sought-after text changes to the replacement text.

TIP

You may now want to check each slide to ensure that the replaced text hasn't confused the text layout in the text box, which sometimes happens when you replace text of one length with text of a substantially different length.

Formatting Text

You can spend hours formatting text. Do you want purple letters, pink letters, or periwinkle letters? Short, tall, or wide? In Helvetica, or Times? Bold, shadowed, or italic? Bullets or no bullets? And in what font size?

To make all these monumental font decisions, first mark the text you wish to change. Then proceed with text formatting using any of the options PowerPoint provides.

To adjust the way your text looks (the formatting), select the text and then choose one of the following methods:

✦ Open the Font dialog box, which offers one-stop shopping for any and all formatting features, by choosing Format⇨Font or by clicking the right mouse button and then clicking Font on the shortcut menu.

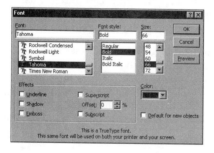

✦ Click a button on the Text Formatting toolbar to change a single formatting feature.

✦ Use a keyboard shortcut to change a formatting feature.

Keyboard Shortcut	Format
Ctrl+B	**Bold**
Ctrl+I	*Italic*
Ctrl+U	<u>Underline</u>
Ctrl+spacebar	Normal (remove formatting)
Ctrl+Shift+F	Font

Keyboard Shortcut	Format
Ctrl+Shift+P	Brings up a dialog box in which you can change point size
Ctrl+Shift+>	Increase point size
Ctrl+Shift+<	Decrease point size

To reset the point size of selected text, click the Font Size area on the Formatting toolbar and type a new point size in the box. Alternatively, you may press the down arrow to reveal a drop-down list of point-size choices.

Note: Ctrl+spacebar clears font attributes, such as bold and underline, but it doesn't reset the font or point size of your text.

Remember that you can change all the following formatting with the Font dialog box as well as the methods discussed in these sections.

Size

To change selected text to an exact size, click the Font Size box on the Text Formatting toolbar and either click a present point size (sizes range from 8 points to 96 points) or type in whatever point size you desire.

Use the Text Formatting toolbar to select a preset point size. Alternatively, you can click inside the font size box one time (the cursor changes to an I-beam) and type in whatever point size you desire. A less convenient option is to make your changes in the Font dialog box, summoned with the Format⇨Font command. As always, making changes to text requires that you first mark the text destined for change.

Here's how to make slight, incremental adjustments to selected text:

 ✦ To increase the font size, press Ctrl+Shift+> or click the Increase Font Size button on the Text Formatting toolbar.

 ✦ To shrink the font size, press Ctrl+Shift+< or click the Decrease Font Size button on the Text Formatting toolbar.

Font

To change the font of selected text, click the arrow next to the Font box on the Text Formatting toolbar and choose a font from the selection that appears.

 PowerPoint places your most frequently used fonts at the beginning of the fonts list. That way, you don't waste time scrolling through the list in search of a font you use all the time.

Color

 Color perks up your text and emphasizes key words and phrases. If you plan to display your PowerPoint presentation as color overheads, 35mm slides or computer output, then invest a little energy in colorizing your text.

Change the color of selected text by clicking the Font Color button on the Drawing toolbar and clicking a color from the palette that appears.

If the font colors that pop up don't suffice, click on More Font Colors for a wider selection of choices. If those colors still don't meet your needs, click the Custom tab and select the one and only perfect shade.

Shadows

 Shadowing text adds a touch of class to your slides. It may also improve readability for some slides by making text characters stand out against their PowerPoint background. Apply a shadow to selected text by clicking the Shadow button.

Embossing

What can I say about embossing except *don't do it!* Embossing text adds a dark shadow below the text and a light shadow above it. Unfortunately, it also changes the text color to the background color, making embossed text darn near impossible to read. It is nice, however, for creating a textured background stamped multiple times with the company name. The text is very subtle and doesn't interfere with information presented in text boxes layered in front of the background.

If you still want to do it, you emboss selected text by choosing Format⇨Font and clicking the Emboss check box.

TIP

Best font, color, and style choices

Here are some formatting tips:

+ **Keep color contrast high.** Dark blue or black text works well on light-colored backgrounds. White or yellow text works well on dark backgrounds.

+ **Keep text point sizes nice and large.** A good rule is to stay above 32 points. *Remember:* The purpose of using PowerPoint is to convey information to your viewers. If they can't read your slides, you won't succeed!

+ **Never use fonts smaller than 20 points in size.** They're just not readable. Use fonts in the 32-point to 72-point range, depending on the selected font. If you need to show more information than will fit on one slide, break it up into two slides.

+ **Avoid using more than two fonts in your presentations.**

+ **Use simple, easy-to-read fonts on all body text.** For example, basic fonts like Arial are much more readable than frilly ones like Algerian.

+ **Reserve funky fonts for titles and use them only when the point size of the title is large enough to maintain the overall clarity of the text.**

+ **Highlight key words or phrases by marking the important text and differing its color to set it off from surrounding text.** White or yellow text can be replaced with light green or light orange; black or dark blue text is replaced well with dark magenta or deep teal.

+ **Shadow text whenever it helps improve the readability of your slides.**

+ **Bold often and never emboss.**

Spell-Checking

Correct spelling is vital in everything you communicate to your audience. If you're going to go to the effort of creating crisp, professional slides, you might as well go to the effort of making sure they're correctly spelled. Besides, there's nothing more embarrassing than misspelling a word and displaying your error to a roomful of watchful colleagues. You can check your spelling after you finish creating your slides or while you're in the process of creating them.

Two tidbits worth mentioning are that PowerPoint can't check grammar — for example, it doesn't flag the word *too* when you really meant to type *to* — and it doesn't check the spelling of embedded objects, like graphs and charts.

After-the-fact

After typing all your text, summon the spell checker to look for spelling mistakes all at once by following these steps:

1. Choose Tools⇨Spelling or click the Spelling button on the Standard toolbar.

2. When PowerPoint finds an error, the program shows the faulty slide and highlights the potentially misspelled word. PowerPoint also recommends possible corrections for your error.

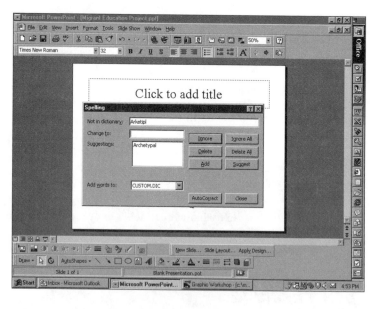

3. Accept one of PowerPoint's corrections and click the Change button, or click Ignore to leave your spelling as is.

If PowerPoint red-flags a word that you know is spelled correctly, click Ignore All to have PowerPoint ignore that word throughout the presentation. ***See also*** "The custom dictionary" in this part.

If you know that you've misspelled a certain word throughout the presentation, click the Change All button and correct all instances of your error in one fell swoop.

4. Repeat Steps 2 and 3 until PowerPoint informs you that the spelling check is complete.

On-the-fly

Besides the standard after-the-fact spell checker, PowerPoint 97 for Windows also offers an on-the-fly spell checker that verifies the spelling of each word immediately after it's typed. The moment you type a word PowerPoint can't understand, it places a wiggly red line under the word in question.

To turn off automatic spell checking:

1. On the Tools menu, click Options, and then click the Spelling tab.

2. Clear the Spelling check box.

The custom dictionary

If you use a nonstandard word often, add it to PowerPoint's custom dictionary. That way, PowerPoint won't nag you about it during spell checks (unless you really have spelled your word incorrectly).

The custom dictionary acts like your own personal version of *Webster's*, so add quirky words to it as often as you please. Whenever PowerPoint incorrectly flags one of your special words, just click the Add words to: custom.dic option.

Undoing Errors

The Undo command is wonderful because it literally undoes your last action. Cleared text reappears. Moved text goes back to its original location. The only thing Undo can't reverse is the passage of time.

Invoke the Undo command in any of three ways:

- ✦ Choose Edit⇨Undo.

- ✦ Click the Undo button on the Standard toolbar.

- ✦ Press Ctrl+Z in Windows.

Undo tracks your 20 most recent actions — but try to fix undo-able errors the minute you notice them. There are a handful of actions on which undo does not work, but PowerPoint typically warns you of this before you execute the action. One such undo-able action is ungrouping certain PowerPoint images into their component objects: This action often cannot be undone such that the image is regrouped into its original composition.

In case you're a finicky sort, PowerPoint also provides a Redo command, which allows you to redo whatever you previously undid.

Invoke the Redo command as follows:

+ Choose Edit⇨Redo.

+ Click the Redo button on the Standard toolbar.

+ Press Ctrl+Y in Windows.

Part V

Drawing Your Own Graphics

Drawing is the quickest and easiest way to add a simple figure or doodle to a PowerPoint slide. The drawing tools let you sketch and colorize basic stuff, like squares, circles, straight lines, wiggly lines, and any combination you can dream up. For really fancy pictures, you may want to forgo tortured-artist efforts and instead use premade PowerPoint drawings called clip art. Using clip art and other multimedia goodies is covered in Part VI.

In this part . . .

✓ Drawing lines

✓ Creating various shapes

✓ Coloring lines and shapes

About the Drawing Toolbar

The Drawing toolbar can be summoned by selecting View⇨
Toolbars⇨Drawing from the menu bar. The Drawing toolbar can be
used in both the Slide and Notes Page views. Each button or menu
on the Drawing toolbar offers a unique tool to assist you in
creating something Picasso would be proud of.

Button	Name
Draw ▾	Draw menu button
	Select Objects button
	Free Rotate button
AutoShapes ▾	AutoShapes menu button
	Line button
	Arrow button
	Rectangle button
	Oval button
	Text box button
	Insert WordArt button
	Fill Color button
	Line Color button
	Font Color button
	Line Style button
	Dash Style button

Button	Name
⇄	Arrow Style button
▣	Shadow button
◨	3-D button

AutoShapes

Clicking the PowerPoint AutoShapes button causes a menu to drop down from which you can choose predrawn line styles and common shapes, like hexagons, banners, moons, and flowchart arrows.

Here's how to use AutoShapes:

1. Click the A̲utoShapes button on the Drawing toolbar. A veritable shopping mall of shapes appears. You can make this AutoShapes dialog box float by clicking the top of the box and dragging it away from the Drawing toolbar.

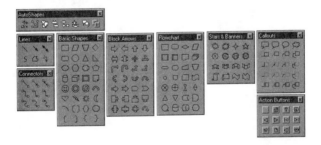

2. Click the AutoShapes category you want:

- **Lines:** Every type of line from straight to swervy. You can also build polygons here.

- **Connectors:** Line segments with strangely shaped end points. Commonly used for road maps and electrical circuits.

- **Basic Shapes:** Hearts, moons, and parallelograms. Get yer Lucky Charms here, laddy!

- **Block Arrows:** Direction arrows such as north, south, and U-turn.

- **Flowchart:** As in, from the wallets of your consumers, into the profit pool of your company, out to the wallets of your shareholders.

- **Stars & Banners:** For patriots and American history teachers.

- **Callouts:** Shapes inside which you type text that describes an image the shape is pointing to or represents what the image is saying or thinking.

- **Action Buttons:** Navigation icons for slide-show and web-based presentations. Some of these little guys resemble buttons on your VCR.

3. Click a shape featured in the category.

4. Draw your chosen shape by clicking your slide and dragging until your AutoShapes object reaches the desired size.

To maintain the same height-to-width proportions as you resize the AutoShapes object, hold down the Shift key while you draw.

Several AutoShapes have special handles that allow you to change the proportions of the AutoShapes object. When drawing objects like parallelograms, you can adjust the handle to tip the parallelogram over a little or a lot, as shown in the following figure.

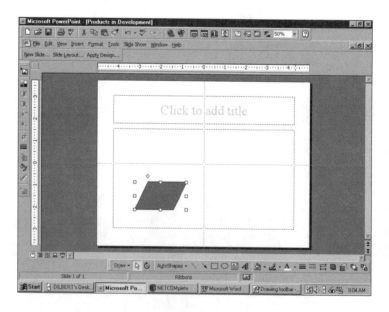

5. Release the mouse button to finish drawing your AutoShapes object. If you made the AutoShapes dialog box float, you can now banish it by clicking the Close button in the upper-right corner.

To change which AutoShape option to use for an object but otherwise keep the color and other attributes you selected for the object, click the object and then choose D<u>r</u>aw➪<u>C</u>hange AutoShape.

See "Lines" in this part for further information about drawing curved and freehand lines with AutoShapes. *See* "Polygons and Freeform Shapes" for more directions about those shapes.

Filling Shapes with Color and Patterns

Coloring within the lines has never been easier. PowerPoint offers you several coloring options, including filling a shape with solid or semitransparent color, shaded blends of two colors, and patterns composed of two colors.

1. Select the shape to be colored by clicking it.

2. Click the Fill Color button and click a color from the box of colors that appears. Note that you can also choose to have no fill, and can access more colors and fill patterns.

Choosing a semitransparent fill option allows your object to have a see-through quality in which lower layers of objects can be partially seen peeking through.

Flipping Objects

Flipping a PowerPoint object creates a mirror image of the object. You can flip in either the horizontal or the vertical direction.

✦ Flipping horizontally makes a flock of westward-flying birds appear as if they've reversed course and started flying eastward.

✦ Flipping vertically makes a moon-bound rocket look as if it's now headed back toward Earth.

Flip a PowerPoint object as follows:

1. Select the object to be flipped by clicking it.

2. To flip the object horizontally, select Draw⇨Rotate or Flip⇨Flip Horizontal, or press the Flip Horizontal button on the Drawing toolbar.

3. To flip the object vertically, select Draw⇨Rotate or Flip⇨Flip Vertical, or press the Flip Vertical button on the Drawing toolbar.

See also "Rotating Objects" in this part.

Grouping, Ungrouping, and Regrouping Objects

Grouping allows you to create and work on simple shapes and then combine them together into a more complex group. By combining, or grouping, several smaller objects into a single larger one, you can treat the grouped object as a single entity, which is particularly helpful when moving or resizing the grouped objects — without grouping, you have to move or resize each little component element one by one.

Create a group as follows:

1. Select the shapes that you want to group by using one of these methods:

• **Shift-click each shape:** Hold down the Shift key and click each individual item that you want as part of the group.

• **Box in all the shapes:** Click near — but not on — the shapes that you want to group. Then drag the mouse to create a picture frame around your shapes. After you complete your frame, release the mouse button. The individual shapes that comprise the art are all selected.

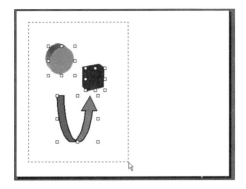

 2. Choose Draw⇨Group or select the Group button from the Drawing toolbar to group your picture.

You may wish to ungroup a grouped object for the purpose of editing elements of the group on an individual basis. Ungroup a grouped object as follows:

1. Select the grouped object by clicking it.

 2. Choose Draw⇨Ungroup or press the Ungroup button from the Drawing toolbar to ungroup the selected object. Once a grouped object has been ungrouped, it identifies each of its component objects by placing resizing handles around each object. You may have to ungroup several times to reach a point where none of objects are grouped.

To regroup a previous grouping:

1. Click any of the objects that were part of the original group.

 2. Choose Draw⇨Regroup or select the Regroup button from the Drawing toolbar. PowerPoint regroups, recalling your previous grouping.

 It's a good idea to group objects that belong in the same layer, particularly when you will be moving layers forwards and backwards to obtain certain physical relationships. *See also* "Layering Objects" in this part for more details.

Inserting WordArt

WordArt is a nifty option that allows you to place fancy, three-dimensional, shadowed text on your slides. The text can even be given a perspective quality, like standing at the *H* looking toward the rest of the letters in the HOLLYWOOD sign.

WordArt text is created from the Drawing toolbar using the WordArt button that summons a collection of WordArt style thumbnails and a special little typing window. After selecting a style and typing in your desired text, your WordArt creation is transferred to your PowerPoint slide as a drawing object. Each WordArt object can be manipulated much like any other drawing object — it can be stretched, skewed, rotated, and filled with any color or texture you choose.

Because WordArt objects do not function like editable text, they don't appear in outline view and they cannot be spell-checked.

Add a WordArt object to a slide as follows:

1. On the Drawing toolbar, click the WordArt button. The WordArt Gallery dialog box appears.

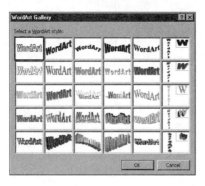

2. Click the thumbnail representing the WordArt style you want to use, and click OK. An Edit WordArt Text dialog box appears.

3. At the Edit WordArt Text dialog box, type your text, select a font and point size, and choose bold or italic formatting options. Click OK. The WordArt text is placed on your slide. To edit your WordArt, use the tools on the Drawing toolbar.

4. For additional WordArt editing tools, summon the WordArt toolbar by selecting View⇨Toolbars⇨WordArt.

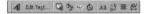

Layering Objects

Layering is a powerful tool for creating perspective and conveying visual relationships. It shuffles the order in which objects appear on-screen, allowing you to choose which objects appear in front and which objects appear behind. For example, you can move a palm tree from in front of the house to behind the house, to show the house more clearly.

Available layering commands include:

 ✦ **Bring to Front:** Brings the selected object (and all other objects with which it is grouped) to the topmost layer of the slide. All other layers will appear behind or underneath the selected object.

 ✦ **Send to Back:** Sends the selected object (and all other objects with which it is grouped) to the bottom layer of the slide. All other layers will appear in front of or on top of the selected object.

 ✦ **Bring Forward:** Brings the selected object (and all other objects with which it is grouped) one layer up or higher on the slide.

 ✦ **Send Backward:** Sends the selected object (and all other objects with which it is grouped) one layer down or lower on the slide.

To change the layer in which an object hangs out:

1. Select the object by clicking it.

2. From the Drawing toolbar, choose a layer button or Draw⇨Order and one of the layering commands.

 Layering tools are located on the Drawing toolbar, but you'll have to perform a couple of steps to get to them. If you frequently need to layer objects, it would be a good idea to add the layering buttons to your Drawing toolbar. Select View⇨Toolbars⇨Customize.

Choose the Commands tab, click Drawing from the Categories list, and then click the Bring to Front button and drag it from the Commands list to the Drawing toolbar. Repeat the procedure for the Send to Back button, the Bring Forward button, and the Send Backward button.

When working with complex drawing objects, you typically want to pair layering operations with grouping operations. First group together objects which belong in a group. Perform this for each group of like objects. Then click each group and move it forward or backward to its proper layer.

Lines

Here's how to draw a straight line:

1. Click the Line button on the Drawing toolbar.

This button shortcut is located on the Drawing toolbar because PowerPoint users require it frequently. You can also find an identical Line button on the Drawing toolbar by selecting AutoShapes⇨Lines and then the Line button.

2. Click and hold where you want the line to start.

3. Drag the mouse to create a line of the desired length and position, and release the mouse when you reach the end of the line.

Holding down the Shift key while drawing your line forces the line to be drawn in 15-degree increments: horizontal; 15, 30, 45, 60, or 75 degrees inclination; or vertical.

To draw a curved line:

1. On the Drawing toolbar, click AutoShapes⇨Lines and then the Curve button.

2. Click your slide where you want the curve to start; then start drawing.

You do not need to hold down the mouse button while drawing.

3. Click each time you want to create a turn or bend in your line. (You can add as many turns as you want.)

4. Double-click to end the line. Double-clicking in close proximity to your starting point creates a closed figure.

To draw a freehand (squiggly) line:

1. On the Drawing toolbar, click AutoShapes⇨Lines and then the Scribble button.

2. Click and drag to draw freehand lines.

3. Release the mouse button to end the line.

See also "AutoShapes" in this part.

Setting line style

After you draw a line, you can change its style — make it thin or thick, solid or dashed, and with or without arrows.

To set line style, click the line that you want to change. Then click one of the following buttons:

✦ **Line Style button:** Choose a new thickness.

The Line Style menu also contains a More Lines command that provides you millions more choices in a dialog box.

✦ **Dash Style button:** Choose a new dash style, if you want your line to appear some other way than solid.

The Dash Style menu lets you select whether your line will appear as a series of dots, short dashes, long dashes, or dots alternating with dashes. Sort of like Morse code!

✦ **Arrow Style button:** Choose arrows as end points for your line.

The Arrow Style menu includes a More Arrows command that provides additional arrow options.

Choosing line colors or patterns

Here's how to alter the color or pattern of a line:

1. Click the line that you want to color. You can also click a shape in order to color the line that creates the shape's boundary.

2. Click the Line Color button and then click a color or a pattern from the pop-up menu.

Choosing a pattern means that your line will have a combination of two colors. These two colors may be patterned together as small dots on a solid background, interweaving lines or other options. It may be difficult to see this pattern clearly if your line is very thin — thicker lines more effectively show patterns.

Lining Up Images with Guides

PowerPoint provides a set of horizontal and vertical crosshairs which aid in lining up objects on your slides. These guides serve the same helpful purpose as grid lines on a sheet of graph paper. When an object is moved close to these crosshairs, it snaps into position so that its center or edge fits snuggly at the crosshairs' point of intersection.

When working in Slide view, activate the guides by choosing View⇨Guides. The guides are initially positioned so that they cross at the geometric center of the slide — a position labeled as (0,0).

Each guide may be moved by clicking on it and dragging it to a new position. As you move a guide up and down, a numerical marker appears indicating the guide's vertical position in inches. As you move a guide left and right, a numerical marker appears which indicates its horizontal position in inches.

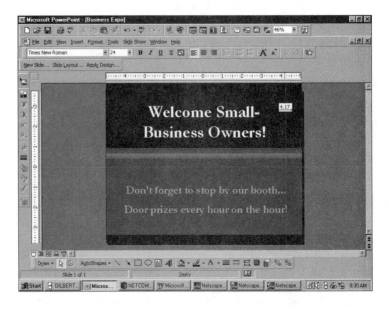

A new guide may be added by clicking an existing guide, pressing Ctrl, and dragging the new guide away. A guide may be deleted by dragging it towards the edge of the slide: Once it reaches the edge, it vanishes.

Lining Up Images with the Ruler

You may never require such precision as PowerPoint's ruler can provide (I never do), but if you're a perfectionist, you can use the ruler to align shapes and images on your slide.

When working in Slide view, activate the ruler by choosing View⇨ Ruler. Two rulers magically appear:

✦ **Horizontal:** The ruler along the top of your slide window. The zero position marks the horizontal halfway location on your slide.

✦ **Vertical:** The ruler along the left side of your slide window. The zero position marks the vertical halfway location on your slide.

Ruler orientation is dependent upon what part of the slide you're working on. The origin (0,0) is located as follows:

✦ **Ouside a text box:** When working outside of a text box, the origin is located at the geometric center of the slide.

✦ **Inside a text box:** When working inside a text box, the origin is located in the upper-left corner of the text box. This means that each text box has its own (0,0) for measuring purposes.

Lining Up Images with Alignment Commands

PowerPoint provides many alignment commands that allow you to set how objects are aligned on your slides. Objects can be aligned with other objects or they can be aligned relative to a slide edge.

You can also arrange or distribute objects so they are spaced equally apart from one another — horizontally, vertically, or relative to the entire slide.

Aligning objects with other objects

To align a set of objects by their left edges or by their right edges:

1. Select the objects you want to align by pressing and holding Shift and clicking on each object.

2. Now to align:

• To align left, click Draw⇨Align or Distribute⇨Align Left on the Drawing toolbar.

- To align right, click Draw⇨Align or Distribute⇨Align Right on the Drawing toolbar.

To align a set of objects horizontally by their centers or vertically by their middles:

1. Select the objects you want to align by pressing and holding Shift and clicking each object.

2. Now to align:

- To align horizontally by their centers, click Draw⇨Align or Distribute⇨Align Center on the Drawing toolbar.

- To align vertically by their middles, click Draw⇨Align or Distribute⇨Align Middle on the Drawing toolbar.

To align objects by their top edges or by their bottom edges:

1. Select the objects you want to align by pressing and holding Shift and clicking on each object.

2. Now to align:

- To align objects by their top edges, click Draw⇨Align or Distribute⇨Align Top on the Drawing toolbar.

- To align vertically by their bottom edges, click Draw⇨ Align or Distribute⇨Align Bottom on the Drawing toolbar.

Aligning objects with the entire slide

To align objects with the entire slide, follow these steps:

1. Select the objects you want to align by pressing and holding Shift and clicking on each object.

2. On the Drawing toolbar, click Draw⇨Align or Distribute⇨ Relative to Slide to place a checkmark next to this option.

3. On the Drawing toolbar, click Draw⇨Align or Distribute⇨ Relative to Slide and then click the option you want to employ in aligning the objects with the slide.

Aligning objects on a grid

Here are a few points to keep in mind when you want to align objects on a grid:

✦ To automatically align objects on an invisible grid, click Draw⇨Snap⇨To Grid on the Drawing toolbar.

✦ To automatically align objects with grid lines that run through the horizontal and vertical edges of other shapes, click Draw⇨Snap⇨To Shape on the Drawing toolbar.

Distributing objects equal distances from one another or relative to the entire slide

To place objects at equal distances from each other or relative to the entire slide, follow these steps:

1. Select the objects you want to align by pressing and holding Shift and clicking each object.

2. To arrange objects equal distances from each other, click Draw⇨Align or Distribute on the Drawing toolbar, and select either the Distribute Horizontally option or the Distribute Vertically option.

3. To arrange objects equal distances from each other relative to the entire slide, make sure the Relative to Slide option is checked. Then click Draw⇨Align or Distribute on the Drawing toolbar, and select either the Distribute Horizontally option or the Distribute Vertically option.

Nudging an object

If you need to move an object just a smidgen, use these nudging steps:

1. Select the object you want to nudge.

2. On the Drawing toolbar, click Draw⇨Nudge, and the direction you wish to nudge the object: up, down, left, or right. Alternatively, you can press an arrow key to nudge a selected object in the desired direction.

Polygons and Freeform Shapes

For those occasions when a regular ol' square or circle just won't do, you may want to create a more elaborate polygon or even a wild freeform shape. Create such beasts thusly:

1. On the Drawing toolbar, click the AutoShapes button, click the Lines button, and then click the Freeform button.

2. Click your slide at the spot where you want to start drawing your object.

3. Release the mouse button and drag to form a straight line segment.

Or

Hold the mouse button down and drag to form a freehand line segment.

Remember: Holding down the Shift key while drawing causes straight lines to form in increments of 15-degree angles.

4. If drawing a straight-line segment, click the mouse button to create a corner and redirect your line. If drawing freehand, release the mouse button to create a corner and redirect your line.

5. Complete your shape by double-clicking. Double-clicking — in close proximity to your starting point— forms a closed figure. Otherwise, you form an open figure.

Your shape automatically fills with color. *See also* "Choosing line colors or patterns" and "Filling Shapes with Color and Patterns" in this part to adjust the line and fill colors and line thickness.

Double-click your finished shape to edit each of its component curves and turns.

Rectangles, Squares, Ovals, and Circles

To draw a rectangular (or square) or oval (or circular) shape, follow these steps:

1. Click the appropriate button:

 • **Rectangle or square:** Click the Rectangle button. To draw a square, hold down the Shift key in Steps 2 and 3 to constrain the proportions.

 • **Oval or circle:** Click the Oval button. To draw a circle, hold down the Shift key in Steps 2 and 3 to constrain the proportions.

2. Click and hold where you want to position the top-left boundary of the shape.

3. Drag to create a shape of the desired shape and size.

4. Release the mouse when your shape has attained the desired proportions.

You can adjust the size and dimensions of your shape by first clicking the created shape and then grabbing and dragging one of its resizing handles.

Rotating Objects

Rotating is turning an object around a central axis. Rotating is particularly useful for making standing objects appear as if they've fallen over: A 90-degree rotation in either direction gets the job done. Rotating is also good for creating a sense of action: A picture of a car on a flat road suddenly conveys motion when you rotate it, with the car appearing either to climb a steep incline or to speed down a sloping hill.

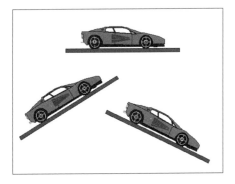

Rotate an object by following these steps:

1. Select the shape to be rotated by clicking it.

2. Now to rotate your object:

- To rotate your object left exactly 90 degrees, choose Draw⇨Rotate or Flip⇨Rotate Left. Rotating left turns the object 90 degrees counterclockwise.

- To rotate your object right exactly 90 degrees, choose Draw⇨Rotate or Flip⇨Rotate Right. Rotating right turns the object 90 degrees clockwise.

- To rotate your shape freely, click the Free Rotate button. Then just grab one of the corner rotation handles on your shape and turn your object clockwise or counterclockwise. Free rotation allows you to rotate your object at any degree angle.

Note: Rotating an object 180 degrees is *not* the same as flipping an object. Rotating 180 degrees turns the object upside-down, whereas flipping creates a mirror image. **See also** "Flipping Objects."

Shadowing Shapes

Shadowing a shape provides you the ability to add depth to the shape by making it appear as if it is casting a shadow. You can adjust how much shadow is generated and where it falls by setting the apparent angle of incidence at which a theoretical "sun" strikes the front of the shape.

To add a shadow to a shape:

1. Click the shape that you want to shadow.

2. Click the Shadow button on the Drawing toolbar and click the shadow style from the box of shadow options that appears.

   Note that this box offers the option of turning off the shadow by pressing No Shadow, and fine-tuning shadow details by pressing Shadow Settings.

3. Click the Shadow button on the Drawing toolbar and click the Shadow Settings button to summon the Shadow Settings toolbar.

   The Shadow Settings toolbar allows you to make adjustments to the shadow color and shadow position. Shadow position buttons cause the applied shadow to be nudged up, down, left, or right.

Three-Dimensional Effects

The 3-D button, which lets you turn flat shapes into 3-D objects without putting those gaudy red and blue glasses over your peepers, is great for showing perspective and for creating a sense of relative position.

Add 3-D effects to a shape as follows:

1. Select the shape by clicking it.

 2. Click the 3-D button on the Drawing toolbar and click a 3-D effect from the box of 3-D effects that appears.

Note that this box offers the option of turning off the 3-D effect by pressing No 3-D, and fine-tuning the three-dimensional details by pressing 3-D Settings.

Clicking 3-D Settings allows you to adjust the tilt, depth, lighting, and texture of the 3-D effects.

Part VI

Adding Multimedia Goodies

Once you get the hang of PowerPoint, mere text and simple backgrounds simply aren't enough to keep you content. The fact that PowerPoint offers you virtually unlimited multimedia capabilities means you'll undoubtedly want to use them! Whether you want to insert simple clip art, professional photos, movie clips of Aunt Mildred, or sound bites of tapping Riverdancers, you'll soon be on your way. This part helps you make your presentations look like symphonies of well-orchestrated graphics, video, and audio.

In this part . . .

- ✔ **Getting rid of multimedia clips**
- ✔ **Adding clip art and pictures**
- ✔ **Locating great multimedia goodies**
- ✔ **Using sound**
- ✔ **Placing video on your slides**

Images: Clip Art and Pictures

Images take the form of either clip art or pictures:

✦ **Clip art:** Line drawings composed of lines, ovals, squares, and all sorts of other shapes. The component shapes of a clip-art image are electronically glued together (in other words, *grouped*) to form the final piece of clip art. A piece of clip art can be broken down into its individual shapes, and each of these shapes can be edited separately.

✦ **Pictures:** Images composed of rows and columns of colored dots (called *pixels*) that combine to form a complete photo-graph-like figure. Pictures cannot be decomposed into their component elements, except with great expertise in a photo-editing program, like PhotoShop. Plan on using a picture as is.

You can find images in the Clip Gallery that comes with PowerPoint, the Clip Gallery Live that PowerPoint 97 users can access on the Internet, and clip-art collections that you can buy in stores or find on the Internet.

Choosing the correct file format

Here are some of the most commonly used image formats that PowerPoint accepts:

✦ **BMP:** Bitmap, a popular Windows format

✦ **EPS:** Encapsulated PostScript, used by top-of-the-line drawing programs

✦ **GIF:** Graphics Interchange Format; common on the Internet

✦ **JPG:** JPEG format; common on the Internet

+ **PCD:** Kodak Photo CD format

+ **PCT:** PICT format; standard Macintosh image file

+ **TIF:** Tagged Image Format; works well for cross-platform images

Adding images from the Gallery

The PowerPoint Clip Gallery is a valuable resource, with thousands of free, high-quality images, sounds, and videos. It's neatly organized into such categories as Academic, Maps, and Transportation, and it provides a helpful little thumbnail sketch of each clip, as you can see in the figure. You can also use the Find keyword-search feature to look for specific images.

 When the Clip Gallery collection becomes dull and passé, PowerPoint offers PowerPoint 97 users a resource called Clip Gallery Live: more free multimedia clips, frequently updated and downloadable off the Internet. To access it, just click the Internet button in the PowerPoint 97 Clip Gallery dialog box. Clip Gallery Live works the same way that the regular Clip Gallery does. And when you click a filename to select an image, that image is downloaded from the Internet and added as a permanent resident to your Clip Gallery.

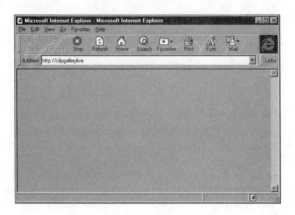

Here's how you drop in an image from the Microsoft Gallery:

1. Move to the slide where you want to add an image. If you want your image to appear on all slides, move to the Slide Master by choosing View⇨Slide Master. *See also* Part II.

2. Choose Insert⇨Picture⇨Clip Art or click the Insert Clip Art button to bring up the Clip Gallery.

3. Click a category and scroll through the images until you locate one you want. Or click the Find button to search for specific image characteristics. When you've settled on an image, click it once to select it. A border appears around the image.

4. To place the picture on your slide, click Insert or double-click the image.

PowerPoint places the image in the middle of your slide. You probably need to move it to a more favorable position. To do so, just click it and drag it to your chosen destination. You also may need to resize the image. *See also* Part II for more information.

If you use the clip-art AutoLayout when you first create a slide, you can call up the Microsoft Clip Gallery by double-clicking in the designated image box. (*Note:* Even though the slide is termed Clip *Art,* it really should be called Clip *Image* because you can add both clip art and pictures.)

See also Part II for more information on AutoLayouts.

Adding images from online sources

To add an image from the Internet to your PowerPoint slide:

1. In your web browser, right-click the image you wish to copy, then select Save Image As from the pop-up menu. Name the image and press Save.

2. Move to the slide where you want to add the image. If you want your image to appear on all slides, move to the Slide Master by choosing View⇨Slide Master. *See also* Part II.

3. Choose Insert⇨Picture⇨From File or click the Insert From File button.

4. In the dialog box that appears, find and click the name of the image you saved in Step 1. Click Insert.

To delete the pasted image, click the image and press Delete. Otherwise, click the image and move it anywhere on the slide you wish. To resize the image, click and drag the handles marking the image borders.

Adding images from other sources

You can buy tons of inexpensive CD-ROMs that offer 2,000 or 3,000 media clips on a single disk. Here's how to add a non-Gallery image to your PowerPoint slide:

1. Go to the slide where you want to add an image. If you want your image to appear on all slides, move to the Slide Master by choosing View⇨Slide Master. *See also* Part II.

2. Choose Insert⇨Picture⇨From File or click the Insert From File button.

3. In the dialog box that appears, click an image from your files and click Insert.

If you're not happy with your chosen image, delete it by clicking it and pressing Delete. Otherwise, click the image and move it to your chosen location. Then resize the image, using the handles marking the image borders.

Moving and resizing your images

PowerPoint adds images to your slides the same way that the cafeteria worker adds food to your tray in the buffet line: glopped down smack dab in the middle. You'll inevitably want to move your picture to a more appetizing location, as well as stretch or shrink your clip art to fit nicely on your slide.

When you insert an image, it appears on your screen as a selected object — with resizing handles surrounding it like a picture frame. If you click outside the image, the handles vanish. Click the image once to make handles reappear. Handles must be visible to move and resize your object.

Move or resize as follows:

+ **Move the image:** Click it once and drag it to a new spot.

+ **Enlarge the image:** Click a corner handle and drag the handle outwards from the object.

+ **Shrink the image:** Click a corner handle and drag the handle in toward the object.

+ **Make the image taller or shorter without changing the width:** Click a top or bottom center handle and drag the handle up or down.

+ **Make the image wider or narrower without changing the height:** Click a left or right center handle and drag the handle horizontally.

Shadowing an image

PowerPoint helps you polish the presentation of your clip images by providing you with a really cool embellishing tool: shadowing. Shadowing can be easily applied around the edges of your image to give it additional depth and make it stand out from the background. You can select the shadow color and position and make adjustments from the Shadow tools on the Drawing toolbar.

Follow these steps to shadow your images:

1. Click the image that you want to shadow.

 2. Click the Shadow button on the Drawing toolbar and click a shadow selection in the box that appears.

Click Shadow Settings to select a shadow color and to nudge the shadow up, down, left or right.

Editing clip art

Very often, you find a clip-art image that's close to meeting your needs, but not perfect. All that's required is a bit of tweaking to whip the clip art into the precise image you need.

The basic process involved in editing a clip art is this:

1. Select the clip art that you want to edit by clicking it.

2. Choose Draw⇨Ungroup from the Drawing toolbar and answer Yes when PowerPoint warns that you're about to convert your clip art to PowerPoint objects.

3. Edit the picture by clicking each element you want changed and then using the drawing tools to adjust the attributes of the element. *See also* Part IV.

4. Regroup the picture by clicking any of the elements in the original group and then choosing Draw⇨Regroup. You can now click and drag your newly edited clip art wherever you like.

Recoloring clip art

Love the clip art but hate the colors? Then do unto your clip art as Ted Turner hath done to many a movie classic: Colorize it. The PowerPoint recolor option allows you to selectively change any or all colors in your chosen clip art.

Recolor clip art as follows:

1. Click the clip art that you want to recolor.

2. Open the Recolor Picture dialog box by clicking the Recolor Picture button on the Picture toolbar. (If you can't find the Picture toolbar, choose <u>V</u>iew⇨<u>T</u>oolbars and click the Picture option to make the toolbar appear.)

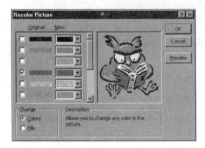

3. In the Original column, click the color that you want to change.

4. Click the New drop-down list box beside your selected original color and click a new color to replace the original color.

5. Repeat Steps 3 and 4 until you've modified every color that you want to change.

6. Click OK to complete the recolor process.

Deleting an image

To remove an image:

1. Select the image by clicking it.

2. Press the Delete key to blow it away.

If you suddenly realize that your deletion was a horrible mistake, choose <u>E</u>dit⇨<u>U</u>ndo, or press Ctrl+Z to get your image back.

Sound

Adding music, sound effects, and other audio snippets to your PowerPoint slides electrifies your presentation more than mere text and images can alone. PowerPoint 97 comes with a small library of sound files you can raid whenever you need a foghorn, phone ring, or rooster. You can find more on the Internet (even beyond Clip Gallery Live!), where you can locate Web sites offering sound clips for virtually every topic imaginable.

 Sound files take up a fair amount of disk space. Each second of sound can occupy 10K or more — small enough to make use of sound but not so small as to go completely nuts with it. Use sound as an embellishment, but don't incorporate 5-minute-long show tunes in your slides, or you'll blow out your processor — and your memory.

Choosing the correct file format

Sound files come in several varieties:

+ **WAV files:** Digitized recordings of real sounds, like a baby crying, a bird tweeting, or a toilet flushing. These files end with the extension WAV.

+ **MIDI files:** Music stored in a form that the sound card's synthesizer can play. These files terminate with an MID extension.

+ **AU files:** Common audio files found on the Internet. These files have the extension AU.

+ **AIFF files:** Also common on the Internet, AIFF files have the extension AIFF.

Adding a sound from the Clip Gallery

Inserting a sound into a PowerPoint presentation is as simple as making your choice and pasting that choice onto a slide. When you run the slide show, you can set up the sounds to play either during slide transitions or at the click of the Sound button. *See also* Part VIII for more information on running the Slide Show.

1. Move to the slide that you want to jazz up with sound.

2. Choose Insert⇨Movies and Sounds⇨Sound from Gallery. The Clip Gallery appears with the Sounds tab activated.

3. Scroll through the list of Clip Gallery sounds until you find the one you're looking for; then click the sound to select it.

4. Click Insert. The sound is pasted on the slide. Notice that a little sound icon appears on the slide to show you that your sound has really been added.

Click to hear the rooster crow

Adding a sound from another source

If you want to insert a sound that has not been cataloged in the
Clip Gallery (such as one you've downloaded from the Internet, or
one you've digitized and stored yourself):

  1. Choose Insert⇨Movies and Sounds⇨Sound from File.

  2. Rummage about your hard drive until you find your stored
    sound; click the sound to select it.

  3. Click OK.

Playing an added sound

To play an added sound while working in Slide view, double-click
the sound icon.

To play the sound during a slide show presentation, single-click
the sound icon whenever it appears on a slide.

You can also cause sounds to play in between slides (during a
slide transition). *See also* Part VIII.

Deleting a sound

To remove a sound:

  1. In Slide view, select the sound icon by clicking it.

  2. Press the Delete key.

If you suddenly realize that your deletion was a horrible mistake, choose <u>E</u>dit⇨<u>U</u>ndo, or press Ctrl+Z to get your sound clip back.

Video

Movies can really enrich a PowerPoint presentation. Placing a movie clip on a slide is similar to adding a sound clip. But because the movie will be both heard *and* seen, you need to give it some room to physically reside on your slide. You should also be aware that the clip itself takes up tons of memory. File sizes are typically 1MB or more, even for a teensy-weensy video snippet. I generally don't use movies except for an occasional wake-up slide or moment of humor.

Choosing the correct file format

Movies come in a variety of file formats, so check that your system is capable of playing the popular ones that you may want to incorporate into your PowerPoint presentations. Common movie formats include:

✦ **QuickTime:** Probably the most prevalent audio/video file format. Playing a QuickTime movie requires no special hardware. You can use either MOV or QT as extensions for QuickTime flicks.

✦ **AVI:** The file type used by Video for Windows. AVI interleaves audio and video which yields a smaller file size than QuickTime. AVI is the extension you'll need.

✦ **MPEG:** MPEG is both a movie file format and a compression/decompression standard. MPEG movies compress to much smaller file sizes than QT and AVI but may require special decoding software and hardware for playback. MPEG, MPG, and MPE are the proper extensions.

AVI is the preferred file format for including movies in your PowerPoint presentations.

Adding a movie from the Clip Gallery

Here's how to add a movie to your slide:

1. Move to the slide where you want to add a movie.

2. Choose <u>I</u>nsert⇨Mo<u>v</u>ies and Sounds⇨<u>M</u>ovie from Gallery. The Clip Gallery appears with the Videos tab selected.

3. Click a movie to select it.

4. Click Insert. The movie is inserted right in the middle of your slide.

5. Resize the movie and reposition it by dragging it to a new location.

Adding a movie from another source

Many commercial CD-ROMs offer short movie clips designed for use in PowerPoint presentations. You can also find several movies available for download from the Internet, although the popularity of streaming video is decreasing the number of movie clips being stored as downloadable, savable files. If you want to add a non-Clip Gallery movie to a slide:

1. Choose Insert⇨Movies and Sounds⇨Movie from File.

2. Search through your hard drive files until you find your stored movie; click the movie to select it.

3. Click OK.

Playing a movie

To play a movie, double-click it when working in Slide view.

When running the slide show presentation, just single-click the movie to start it playing.

During a PowerPoint presentation, you can make a movie play automatically when you arrive at the slide where it resides. *See also* Part VIII for details.

Deleting a movie clip

To remove a movie clip:

1. Select the clip by clicking it.

2. Press the Delete key.

If you decide that you made a mistake, choose Edit⇨Undo, or press Ctrl+Z, to get your movie clip back.

Part VII

Showing Your Business Savvy

In the world of art, a picture is worth a thousand words. In the world of business, a picture of your data — in charts, graphs, equations, spreadsheets, or tables — is worth 1,000 bucks. This part addresses how to create the best darn graphs and organizational charts for display in PowerPoint, along with how to insert complex equations and spreadsheets into your presentation with minimal effort.

In this part . . .

✔ **Building a graph**

✔ **Creating an organizational chart**

✔ **Importing spreadsheets and tables**

✔ **Using the Equation Editor**

Incorporating Graphs

The PowerPoint graphs give you a tool for taking numerical information and converting it into a lovely graph. You can choose from pie graphs, bar graphs, and even some exotic things called *cone graphs,* not to be confused with the Coneheads.

Note: One key point of clarification: Microsoft refers to *graph* and *chart* interchangeably — a habit I consider incredibly confusing. This book always refers to an object built by Microsoft Graph as a *graph* and always refers to an organizational chart as a *chart.* And never the twain shall meet.

Adding a slide with a graph placeholder

To create a new slide on which you intend to place a graph, follow these steps:

1. In Slide view or Slide Sorter view, move to the location in your presentation where you want to insert a new slide with a graph.

 2. Click the New Slide button on the Common Tasks toolbar.

3. Choose an AutoLayout option that includes a graph, and click OK. (Unfortunately, the name tag refers to the graph as a *chart.* Just ignore it.)

4. Double-click the graph placeholder to open Microsoft Graph. Microsoft Graph creates a sample graph accompanied by a sample datasheet.

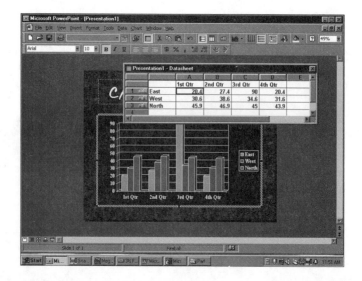

5. Input your own data to the datasheet, which works like a spreadsheet. *See also* "Using the datasheet."

6. Click outside the graph area to return to the slide. The graph is redrawn with the data you entered in the datasheet.

Adding a graph to a current slide

To add a graph to a slide already in your presentation:

1. Move to the slide where you want to add a graph.

 2. To place a sample graph and datasheet on your slide, click the Insert Chart button on the Standard toolbar or choose Insert⇨Chart.

3. Replace the data in the sample datasheet with your actual information. (*See also* "Using the datasheet.")

4. Click outside the graph area to return to the slide. The graph is redrawn with the data you input to the datasheet.

You probably need to resize the graph or move the graph and other objects around to improve the look and readability of the slide.

Using the datasheet

Microsoft Graph uses data you supply in the datasheet to construct the graph that ultimately ends up (looking beautiful) on your slide. The datasheet functions as a simple spreadsheet, providing rows and columns for you to insert your data. Rows are designated by numbers, and columns are designated by letters; each data point you enter is cubbyholed in a unique cell of the datasheet.

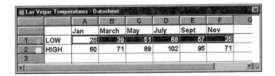

Here are a few things to note:

+ The datasheet reserves the first row and column for headings to label the resulting graph, so don't attempt to enter any numerical data in these cells.

✦ The datasheet does not allow you to perform certain spreadsheet operations, such as using formulas. So if you require something more powerful — like Microsoft Excel — first create and save the spreadsheet in your program of choice. Then choose Insert⇨Object from the PowerPoint main menu to include the spreadsheet on your slide.

✦ Depending on how much room you require for each cell, you may want to adjust the column width by choosing Format⇨Column Width. Column width is just for ease of use when working in the datasheet — adjusting column widths will not affect the graph itself.

✦ You may also want to reformat the type of numbers in the datasheet by choosing Format⇨Number and selecting from options such as Percent, Scientific, and Currency. As with any spreadsheet-style program, using the Format command assists you in entering and manipulating a variety of number types.

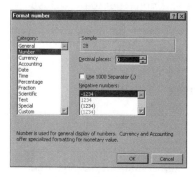

Graph options

After filling your datasheet with numbers, wave the magic wand and magically transform those numbers into a graph suitable for display. Microsoft Graph offers you 14 graph types, from the obvious (line, scatter) to the sublime (doughnut, radar). It also offers you a handful of unusual, custom graph types in case none of the standard types strikes your fancy. Try out several graph types for your data before settling on one that best conveys the information to your audience.

To choose a graph type after completing your datasheet:

1. Double-click the graph to activate the Microsoft Graph program. If you're already working in Microsoft Graph, just single-click the graph to select it.

2. Choose <u>C</u>hart⇨Chart <u>T</u>ype to open the Chart Type dialog box.

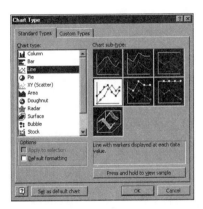

3. Choose a graph type by clicking it. You may also click an option in the Chart sub-<u>t</u>ype area, which offers variations on the theme.

4. To obtain a thumbnail preview of how your data will appear in a selected graph type, click the Press and Hold to <u>V</u>iew Sample button.

5. Click OK to accept your choice.

 A shortcut method for selecting a graph type is to click the Chart Type button on the menu bar. A small palette appears, allowing you to choose from the most commonly used graph types.

Labeling a graph

After you insert the graph type of your choice on your slide, the final step in completing the graph is adding labels: a title, labels for the axes, and a deciphering legend.

Add labels to your graph as follows:

1. Double-click the graph to activate the Microsoft Graph program. If you're already working in Microsoft Graph, just single-click the graph to select it.

2. Choose <u>C</u>hart⇨Chart <u>O</u>ptions to open the Chart Options dialog box. Use these six tabs to format your graph:

Axis labels   Title   Legend

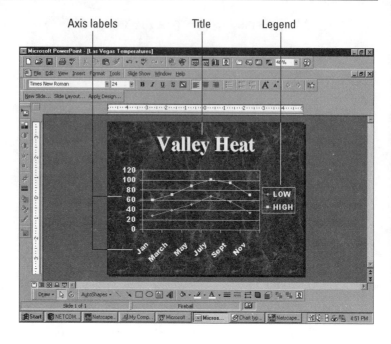

- **Titles:** Add both an overall title for the graph and titles for each axis. To adjust the font and size of a title, exit Chart Options by clicking Cancel in the Chart Options dialog box, click the title you want to change, and then choose Format⇨Font to make your adjustments.

- **Axes:** Hide or show the labels you've given the data on the datasheet.

- **Gridlines:** Activate and deactivate the lines that appear with the chart for the purpose of helping the audience better visualize the position of the plotted data.

- **Legends:** Turn on/off and position a legend.

- **Data Labels:** Display the actual numerical data on-screen for each data point in your datasheet. With few exceptions, choose None for displaying labels — the extra text makes the graph appear messy.

- **Data Tables:** If you want to show actual data, choose the Data Table option as an accompaniment for your graph.

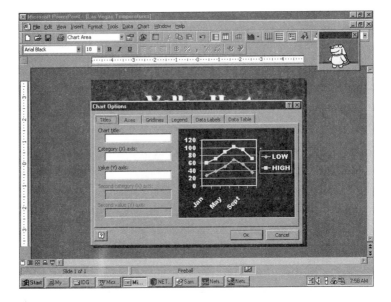

Moving and resizing a graph

As Microsoft Graph may or may not position your newly created graph in the appropriate location, you'll probably want to move the graph and possibly resize it, too.

✦ **To move a graph:** Click and drag the graph — not on the sizing handles — to move it to a new destination.

✦ **To resize a graph:** Click it and then pull on one of its handles. Holding down the Shift key while resizing maintains the proportions of the graph. Be aware that resizing may alter text readability.

Incorporating Organizational Charts

To show the relationship among several entities without whipping out index cards and strands of yarn and creating your own little pin-up organizational chart, call on PowerPoint and one of its handy little subprograms: Microsoft Organizational Chart.

Adding a slide with an organizational chart

To create a new slide on which you intend to place an organizational chart:

1. In Slide view or Slide Sorter view, move to the location in your slide stack where you want to insert a new slide with an organizational chart.

2. Click the New Slide button on the Common Tasks toolbar.

3. Choose an AutoLayout that includes an organizational chart and click OK.

4. Double-click the org chart placeholder to open Microsoft Organizational Chart. The program creates a sample chart from which you will construct your own organizational chart.

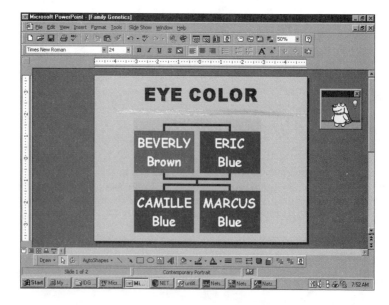

5. Input your own information to the organizational chart. *See also* "Working with Organizational Chart boxes and connectors."

6. Choose File⇨Exit and Return to go back to the slide. The chart is redrawn with the information you supplied.

Adding an organizational chart to the current slide

To add an organizational chart to a slide already in your presentation:

1. Move to the slide where you want to add an organizational chart.

2. To place a sample organizational chart on your slide, click the Insert Organizational Chart button on the Standard toolbar; or choose Insert⇨Object, click MS Organizational Chart 2.0, and click OK.

3. Replace the data in the sample organizational chart with your actual information.

4. Go back to the slide by choosing File⇨Exit and Return, or by clicking the X in the upper-right corner of the Organizational Chart window and answering Yes when asked whether you want to update the organizational chart object. The chart is redrawn with the data you input to the datasheet.

Working with Organizational Chart boxes and connectors

Microsoft Organizational Chart offers you a variety of box and connector styles for showing the relationship between different entities. Here's the skinny on what's available:

✦ **Manager:** A top-level box.

✦ **Subordinate:** A box representing a person who reports to a manager.

✦ **Co-worker:** Anyone who works laterally, in a peer relationship, with another worker. Co-worker boxes can represent subordinates who report to different managers.

✦ **Assistant:** The Assistant's box connects on an equal level to the box of the person he or she is assisting.

✦ **Group:** Includes all the boxes reporting to a manager.

✦ **Connecting line:** The line that attaches two boxes.

Adding and deleting boxes on an organizational chart

To add a new box to your organizational chart:

1. From the box selection bar below the Organizational Chart menu bar, click the type of box (Manager, Subordinate, and so on) that you want to add.

2. On your organizational chart, click the box to which you want to attach your new box.

3. Fill in your newly added box, pressing Enter to start each new line.

4. Click outside the newly added box to complete its addition to the chart.

To delete a box from your organizational chart:

1. Click the box that you want to delete.

2. Press the Delete key or choose Edit➪Cut.

Choosing a group style

The group style of your organizational chart defines how your boxes are positioned relative to one another — kind of like planning the seating arrangement for a holiday dinner. Choosing a group style can be useful in helping arrange an organizational chart to neatly fit the confined area of a PowerPoint slide. For example, a group style can indicate whether a group of coworker boxes is arranged horizontally or vertically. An existing group style can also be changed by selecting a group of boxes on the organizational chart and applying a new group style.

TIP

You can also employ several group styles within the same chart so that each branch of the chart can be drawn custom-tailored to your needs.

Apply a group style to your chart as follows:

1. Hold down the Shift key while clicking each box that you want to include in the new group style.

If you want to include the entire chart in the new group style, choose Edit➪Select➪All, or press Ctrl+A.

2. Click the Styles menu and choose a group style. The group style is applied to your selected boxes.

Moving boxes on an organizational chart

Move a box from one position to another with these steps:

1. Click the box that you want to move.

2. Drag the box to its new position, making sure it covers the box that indicates its new Manager or its new Co-worker.

The new Manager or Co-worker box highlights to let you know you're in the right spot.

3. Release the box, and it automatically repositions in its new location. All subordinates reporting to the repositioned box move as well.

Formatting the organizational chart

As a finishing touch for your organizational chart, you'll probably want to color certain boxes, thicken a few connecting lines, or alter the font and text size to improve readability.

Format boxed material presented in your organizational chart as follows:

1. Click the box that you want to format. To format multiple boxes, hold down the Shift key while clicking each box. To format all boxes in the entire chart, choose Edit⇨Select⇨All, or press Ctrl+A.

2. Click the Text menu and click a formatting option (font, color, or alignment of the text in the boxes).

3. Click the Boxes menu and click an option for formatting the boxes themselves (color, shadow, border style, border color, and border line style of the selected boxes).

Format the background color of your organizational chart by choosing Chart⇨Background Color and clicking a color in the palette.

Format connecting lines of your organizational chart as follows:

1. Click the connecting line that you want to format. To format multiple connecting lines, hold down the Shift key while clicking each line. To format all connecting lines in the entire chart, choose Edit⇨Select⇨Connecting Lines.

2. Click the Lines menu and click a formatting option (thickness, style, or color of your chosen connecting lines).

Importing Business Files from Other Sources

You have a few options to spruce up your business presentations, without having to redo a lot of work. Just try importing spreadsheets from Excel or Word documents.

Spreadsheets (from Excel)

For occasions when you want to include a more detailed spreadsheet on your PowerPoint slide, you can choose to insert a Microsoft Excel spreadsheet. Excel offers you greater functionality and data manipulation capabilities than the more basic datasheet provided as part of Microsoft Graph.

Insert an Excel spreadsheet as follows:

1. On the Standard toolbar, click the Insert Excel Worksheet button.

2. Fill the spreadsheet cells and adjust column widths, using standard Excel procedures.

3. Click outside the spreadsheet to exit.

Tables (from Word)

Inserting massive quantities of text on your PowerPoint slides is rarely a good idea. But if you're forced to present text-intensive information, organize that information into a tidy Word table. Here's how:

1. On the Standard toolbar, click the Insert Word Table button.

2. Click the mouse where you want the upper-left corner of the table to appear; then drag the mouse and release it to select the size table you want to add.

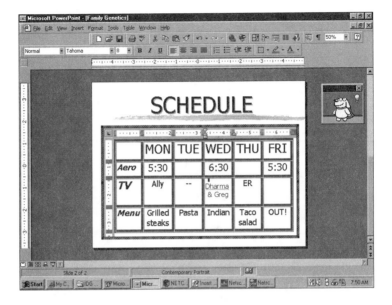

3. Fill the table cells and adjust column widths, using standard Word table procedures.

4. Click the Border button to add borders to your complete table.

 5. Click outside the table to exit.

Recording and Printing Meeting Minutes and Action Items

During a slide show, you have the option of recording minutes, action items, audience comments, and brainstorming ideas directly to your PowerPoint presentation. PowerPoint's Meeting Minder function makes it all possible. Meeting Minder lets you record action items as-you-present, and collect all action items for display on a new slide. The slide of action items is placed at the end of your slide show, providing you and your audience a concise "to-do" list as you end your presentation. Action items and minutes can be saved to a new Word document for later editing, printing, and distribution.

Taking notes during a slide show

Follow these steps to jot down notes or other written records during your presentation:

1. Working in Slide Show view, right-click the mouse, and click Meeting Minder or Speaker Notes.

A Meeting Minder box or Speaker Notes box appears accordingly.

2. Click in the box, type your minutes or notes, and click Add.

Creating a list of action items during a slide show

If you want to add a list of action items while you're presenting your slide show, follow these steps:

1. Working in Slide Show view, right-click the mouse, click Meeting Minder, and click the Action Items tab.

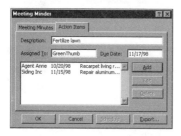

2. Click in the box, type one action item, and click Add.

3. Repeat Step 2 for each separate item.

Action items will be collected and listed on a new slide placed at the end of your presentation. The new slide will be titled, "Action Items."

Saving meeting minutes and action items to a Word document

Suppose you want to add meeting minutes and action items to a Word document. You're in luck! Just follow these steps:

1. Working in Slide Show view, right-click the mouse, click Meeting Minder, and click the Meeting Minutes or Action Items tab.

2. Type in the box to record minutes or action items throughout the meeting. *See also* "Taking notes during a slide show," and "Creating a list of action items during a slide show."

3. Click Export.

4. Click the Send meeting minutes and action items to Microsoft Word check box, and click Export Now.

Microsoft Word opens and copies the exported Meeting Minder contents to a new document.

Working with Equation Editor

Equation Editor is a nifty little program that makes a (fairly) simple task of generating superscripts, square roots, absolute values, summations, and a whole slew of other mathematical symbols.

Note: This program ships with Microsoft Office. It's probably already installed on your system, but if not, insert your Office CD-ROM and select Start⇨Settings⇨Control Panel⇨Add/Remove Programs. From the Office Setup screen, proceed with installing the Equation Editor. For more details on installing new programs, please see *Windows 95 For Dummies Quick Reference,* 3rd Edition, by Greg Harvey (IDG Books Worldwide, Inc.).

So slap an equation on a slide as follows:

1. In Slide view, move to the slide where you want to add an equation.

2. Choose Insert⇨Object to bring up the Insert Object dialog box.

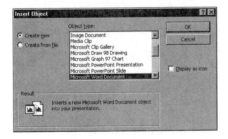

3. Click Microsoft Equation 3.0 (you may have to scroll down through the list) and click OK. The Equation Editor window appears.

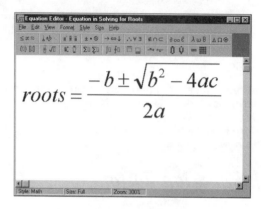

4. Type your equation, using the standard keys on the keyboard and the buttons on the Equation toolbar (at the top of the window). This step is easier said than done; you may have to tinker a bit.

If necessary, use the Style menu to format the numerical characters in your equation. Style options consist of Math, Text, Function, Variable, Greek, Symbol, and Matrix-Vector. Equation Editor normally performs this formatting task for you, as it presents you with preformatted templates in which you type your numbers and variables. You may occasionally need to intervene with adjustments to improve the look of your creation so that it conveys the intended mathematical meaning.

5. Choose File➪Exit and Return to close Equation Editor and add the equation to your slide.

6. Drag the handles of the newly added equation to adjust its size on your slide.

You may also want to change the background color of the equation or of the slide itself to make the equation more readable. *See also* Part III for additional information on changing background colors.

To edit an equation on a slide, simply double-click the equation to restart the Equation Editor program. Then make your changes and choose File➪Exit to return to PowerPoint.

Part VIII

Showing the Presentation

After you create your slides, you probably want to rearrange them and put a few finishing touches on the way the information is presented. You may want to use cool animation for adding text and pictures to each slide. Or you may want to incorporate some hyperlinks or buttons to your slides to give you dynamic control over how you or the user moves through the presentation. Lastly, you require some means of displaying your finished slide show to your anticipating audience. This part tells you how to polish off that presentation and get on with the show!

In this part . . .

- ✔ Working in Slide Sorter view
- ✔ Transitioning and animating your slides
- ✔ Hyperlinking and adding buttons to your slides
- ✔ Setting up and showing your presentation

About Slide Sorter View

During the slide-construction process, you spend most of the time working in Slide view. The limitation of Slide view, however, is that you can't peruse your entire batch of slides simultaneously. Enter Slide Sorter view.

Slide Sorter view works on the same principle as a light table used for 35mm slides: It allows you to inspect all the slides in your collection at once and sort them into a sequence that you feel will work best for the presentation.

The Slide Sorter toolbar provides you complete control over everything from how each slide appears and disappears (slide transitions) to how text bullet items and pictures make their entrance onto each slide.

To use Slide Sorter view:

1. From any view, at any slide in your presentation, click the Slide Sorter view button, located with the other view buttons in the lower-left corner of the screen. Or choose View⇨Slide Sorter.

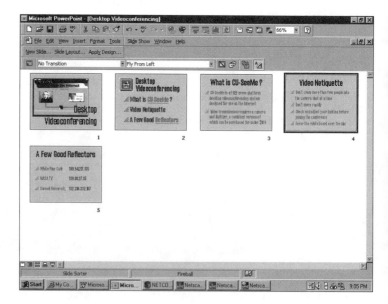

If your entire slide stack doesn't fit on-screen, use the scroll bars to scroll through your slides.

Also, you can adjust the total number of slides visible in Slide Sorter view by clicking the Zoom drop-down list box on the Standard toolbar.

2. Click the appropriate button on the Slide Sorter toolbar that appears.

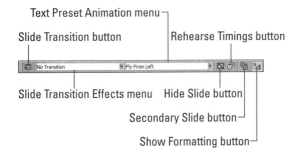

- **Slide Transition button:** Opens Slide Transition dialog box. *See* "Adding Slide Transitions" later in this part.

- **Slide Transition Effects menu:** Opens menu of slide transitions. These transitions define how, during a slide show, one slide leaves the screen and the next slide appears in its place.

- **Text Preset Animation menu:** Opens menu of text-animation options. These animations define how, during a slide show, lines of body text are added to an on-screen slide. This menu provides a complete selection of text animation options, but applies to text only — not to other objects on the slide.

- **Hide Slide button:** Toggles to hide/show a slide during a slide show. The Hide Slide function is useful when you want to customize a show by displaying only a subset of slides in the presentation. Slides that you do not want to show can be hidden — but they are not deleted.

- **Rehearse Timings button:** Activates Slide Show with Rehearsal dialog box. When running a slide show in standalone mode — like at an information kiosk — you have the option of allowing PowerPoint to advance the slides, in sequence, at any time interval you choose. Rehearse Timings lets you set display durations for each slide.

- **Summary Slide button:** Automatically creates a summary slide from slide titles. This slide follows the formatting of the Slide Master, and is comprised of bullets consisting of the titles of all selected slides. The summary slide is inserted in front of the first selected slide, and may therefore be more aptly named an agenda slide.

- **Show Formatting button:** Toggles to hide/show complete slide layouts or titles only in Slide Sorter view. The purpose of hiding slide layouts is to save time when building the Slide Sorter view. If you choose to Show Formatting, it will take a longer period of time to layout your slides in this view.

Return to Slide view at any time by double-clicking any slide in the Slide Sorter, or by single-clicking a slide and clicking the Slide view button in the lower-left corner of the screen.

Moving slides around in Slide Sorter view

Moving and reordering slides is a snap when working in the Slide Sorter. Here's how to shuffle your slides around:

1. Click the slide that you want to move. To move multiple slides as a group, hold down the Shift key while clicking each slide that you want included in the group.

2. Drag the slide (or slide group) to position it between two other slides in the stack. A long, blinking cursor symbol indicates where the slide (or slide group) will be repositioned.

3. Release the mouse button. The slide or slides are repositioned, and the entire stack of slides is renumbered accordingly.

Adding and duplicating slides

To add a new slide:

1. In Slide Sorter view, click between the two slides where you want the new slide inserted. The long, blinking cursor marks the spot for insertion.

2. Click the New Slide button and choose an AutoLayout for the new slide. The new slide is added at the cursor.

To add a slide from another presentation:

1. In Slide Sorter view, click between the two slides where you want the slide from another presentation to be inserted. The long, blinking cursor marks the spot for insertion.

2. Switch to the other presentation, and move to the Slide Sorter view. Click the slide you want to copy and add to your original presentation.

3. Copy the selected slide by selecting Edit⇨Copy or pressing Ctrl+C.

4. Return to your original presentation, and select Edit⇨Paste or press Ctrl+V.

To duplicate a slide:

1. In Slide Sorter view, click the slide that you want to clone.

2. Choose Edit⇨Duplicate. The duplicate slide is inserted immediately after the original slide.

See also "Moving slides around in Slide Sorter view" for details on moving the position of your added or duplicated slides.

Deleting slides

Some deleting instructions:

✦ To delete a slide, click the slide and press Backspace or Delete.

✦ To delete multiple slides, hold down the Shift key while clicking each slide that you want to delete; then press Backspace or Delete.

✦ To retrieve a deleted slide, choose Edit⇨Undo Delete Slide.

The slide stack is renumbered according to the total number of deletions you execute.

Adding Animation

Animation is the term PowerPoint gives to making text and pictures appear on your slides. PowerPoint animation is not as elaborate as *Toy Story,* but it's a heck of a lot better than those antique cartoon flip books. If you've worked with older versions of PowerPoint, you probably remember this process as "building the text" — and that you previously had no accommodations for animating pictures.

You have more than 50 animation effects to choose from, but if I were you, I'd pick a single good one and stick with it. Establishing an easy-to-follow pattern for revealing text will keep your audience focused on what you're saying rather than how you're saying it. My favorite effects are Fly from Right and Fly from Bottom. Avoid Random Effects, as the variation from slide to slide will frustrate your audience.

Animating text

Establish the animation of text on a slide as follows:

1. Click the Slide Sorter view button to bring up the Slide Sorter toolbar. *See also* "About Slide Sorter View" earlier in this part.

2. Click the slide where you want to add text animation. To apply the same animation to all slides, choose Edit⇨Select All.

3. Click a text animation effect from the Text Preset Animation menu on the Slide Sorter toolbar. Text animation options include:

- **No effect**

- **Appear**

- **Fly:** Options consist of Bottom, Left, Right, Top, Bottom-Left, Bottom-Right, Top-Left, or Top-Right

- **Blinds:** Options consist of Horizontal or Vertical

- **Box:** Options consist of In or Out

- **Checkerboard:** Options consist of Across or Down

- **Crawl:** Options consist of Bottom, Left, Right, or Top

- **Dissolve**

- **Flash Once:** Options consist of Fast, Medium, or Slow

- **Peek From:** Options consist of Bottom, Left, Right, Top

- **Random Bars:** Options consist of Horizontal or Vertical

- **Random Effects**

- **Spiral**

- **Split Horizontal:** Options consist of In or Out

- **Split Vertical:** Options consist of In or Out

- **Stretch:** Options consist of Across, From Bottom, From Left, From Right, or From Top

- **Strips:** Options consist of Left-Down, Left-Up, Right-Down, Right-Up

- **Swivel**

- **Wipe:** Options consist of Down, Left, Right, Up

- **Zoom:** Options consist of In, In From Screen Center, In Slightly, Out, Out From Screen Bottom, or Out Slightly

Slide Sorter view tags each slide that you use text animation on with a miniature Animation Effects button as a reminder that the slide is animated.

Animation Effects tag

More options: Using Preset Animation for text and objects

You can add greater pizzazz and flexibility to your slide animation by using Preset Animation. Preset Animation offers some really cool animation effects — most complemented with sounds — to animate both text and pictures on your slides. It differs from the preceding section, "Animating text" in that more than text alone can be animated. It also differs from the following section, "Custom animation," which offers significantly more animation options but requires much more time and effort than using Preset Animation.

Preset Animation can be added to your slides by pressing buttons on the Animation Effects toolbar, or by executing commands at the Slide Show⇨Preset Animation pop-up menu from the menu bar. The Animation Effects toolbar offers a bit more functionality than the Preset Animation menu, in that the toolbar also lets you determine the order in which you animate slide objects.

Here's how to use Preset Animation:

1. Specify an entire slide for animation by clicking the Slide Sorter view button and clicking the target slide.

Specify individual slide elements for animation by clicking the Slide view button and clicking the target text or object.

2. To select Preset Animation, choose Slide Show⇨Preset Animation form the menu bar. You may alternatively bring up the Animation Effects toolbar by clicking the Animation Effects button on the Standard toolbar.

3. Animate the target slide or slide element by choosing a Preset Animation menu option, or clicking a button on the Animation Effects toolbar.

Clicking Custom Animation opens a dialog box that gives you total control over animation effects. (*See also* "Custom animation.")

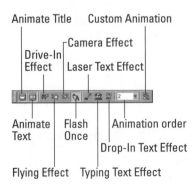

Animate Title   Custom Animation

Drive-In   ⌐Camera Effect
Effect   Laser Text Effect

Animate   Flash   Animation order
Text   Once
Drop-In Text Effect

Flying Effect   Typing Text Effect

Button or Menu Item	What Choosing this Item does
Animate Title (toolbar only)	Applies animation effect to the title
Animate Text (toolbar only)	Applies animation effect to selected text object
Drive-In Effect	Object or text flies in from the right, accompanied by an Indianapolis 500 car screech
Flying Effect	Object or text flies in from the left, accompanied by a whoosh sound like a flying pizza
Camera Effect	Object or text boxes out from its center, accompanied by a camera sound
Flash Once	Object or text flashes on-screen, then disappears
Laser Text Effect	Text shoots on-screen from upper right-hand corner, one letter at a time, accompanied by pulsing laser sound
Typing Text Effect	Text types on-screen, one letter at a time, accompanied by a typewriter sound
Drop-In Text Effect	Text falls into place from top of screen, one word at a time
Animation Order (toolbar only)	Sequences the order in which objects are animated during the slide show
Custom Animation (toolbar only)	Opens the Custom Animation dialog box

Custom animation

The Custom Animation dialog box allows you to be an absolute ruler over the Kingdom of PowerPoint Animation. You wield total decision-making power over how and when all slide elements are animated.

Creating custom animation typically requires more time than I'm willing to spend on controlling such fine details. I recommend it only for the hard-core Type A's among you.

Follow these steps:

 1. Click the Slide view button and move to the slide that you want to animate.

2. Click the text element or picture to be animated.

3. Choose Slide Show⇨Custom Animation to bring up the Custom Animation dialog box.

4. Click the Timing tab.

5. In the Start Animation area, press the Animate radio button, then choose On Mouse Click or Automatically.

Choosing Automatically requires you to also select the number of seconds after the previous slide show event you want the animation to occur.

6. Click the Effects tab.

7. In the Entry animation and sound area click an animation and click a sound from the two drop-down list boxes.

Also complete the After Animation area by selecting what happens to the animated object after the animation has been executed. Options are Don't Dim, Hide after Animation, Hide on Next Mouse Click, and More Colors. More Colors allows you to choose a color to which animated text will change after it has been animated.

8. If you are animating a text object, click an option in the Introduce text area. The options in the drop-down list that appears are All at once, By word, and By letter.

9. If you are animating a chart or graph, press the Chart Effects tab in the Custom Animation dialog box, and select how you want your chart animated.

10. If you are animating a movie object, press the Play Settings tab in the Custom Animation dialog box, and select how you want your chart animated.

11. Tweak any other animation effects as needed.

12. Click the Preview button to see how your selections look, sound, and move. Click OK when you're satisfied.

Adding Slide Transitions

Slide transitions describe how slides enter and exit as you present your on-screen slide show. You can select to use one type of transition consistently throughout your entire presentation, or you can choose unique transitions for individual slides. You can also adjust the speed at which a transition occurs — slow, medium, or fast — and even cause a sound to play as the transition takes place. PowerPoint offers the following transitions for use during your presentation:

✦ **No Transition:** The default transition

✦ **Blinds:** Options consist of Horizontal or Vertical

✦ **Box:** Options consist of In or Out

✦ **Checkerboard:** Options consist of Across or Down

✦ **Cover:** Options consist of Down, Left, Right, Up, Left-Down, Left-Up, Right-Down, or Right-Up

✦ **Cut**

✦ **Cut Through Black**

✦ **Dissolve**

✦ **Fade Through Black**

✦ **Random Bars:** Options consist of Horizontal or Vertical

✦ **Random Transition**

✦ **Split:** Options consist of Horizontal In, Horizontal Out, Vertical In, or Vertical Out

✦ **Strips:** Options consist of Left-Down, Left-Up, Right-Down, or Right-Up

✦ **Uncover:** Options consist of Down, Left, Right, Up, Left-Down, Left-Up, Right-Down, or Right-Up

✦ **Wipe:** Options consist of Down, Left, Right, or Up

You can add transitions to your presentation using either the Slide Transition Effects menu or the Slide Transition dialog box. Creating transitions with the menu is the more expedient process, while creating transitions with dialog box allows you greater control over transition details like speed and sound.

To add transitions to your presentation using the Slide Transition Effects menu:

1. In Slide Sorter view, click on a slide where you want to add a transition.

   To select multiple slides, hold down Shift as you click. To select all slides, choose Edit⇨Select All or press Ctrl+A.

2. Press the arrow tab on the Slide Transition Effects menu and select a transition.

   Each slide is tagged with a transition effects marker indicating a transition has been added.

Transition Effects tag

In Slide Sorter view, pressing a slide's transition effects tag causes a thumbnail preview of the transition to play.

To add transitions to your presentation using the Slide Transition dialog box:

1. In Slide view or Slide Sorter view, click on a slide where you want to add a transition.

   To select multiple slides in Slide Sorter view, hold down Shift as you click. To select all slides in either view, choose Edit⇨Select All or press Ctrl+A.

2. Summon the Slide Transition dialog box by selecting Slide Show⇨Slide Transition from the menu bar.

3. In the Effect area of the Slide Transition dialog box, choose a transition from the drop-down menu box. Also choose a transition speed: slow, medium, or fast.

A thumbnail preview shows how your choices will appear in the slide show.

4. In the Advance area, choose whether you want the transition to occur On Mouse Click or Automatically. Choosing Automatically also requires you to enter the number of seconds before the transition will be performed.

5. You may ignore the Sound Area of the Slide Transition dialog box, or you may select a sound for the drop-down menu box. Loop until next sound causes the sound to play repeatedly until another sound in the presentation is played.

6. Press Apply to accept and apply your choices, or Apply to All if you want your choices applied to every slide in the presentation.

PowerPoint allows you to apply any transition to any slide. However, if you want to look like a real PowerPoint pro, I encourage you to pick one transition type and apply it consistently throughout your entire presentation. Don't use any transition with the adjective *random* in its name. Be creative, but don't overdo it such that your audience pays more attention to your wacky transitions than to the information on your slides. You'll appear most professional if you choose something elegant, like a straight cut, a fade through black or a dissolve, cover, uncover, wipe, or strip. Please avoid the venetian blind and checkerboard effects — they will totally annoy your audience!

Note: For those of you delivering your presentations over compressed video technologies — like desktop video — don't bother with transitions at all. Compression pretty much obliterates the motion of a transition.

Adding Action Buttons

PowerPoint 97 offers you some way-cool *action buttons* that you
can click during a slide show to perform certain specialized
functions. You can define buttons to perform a range of functions,
such as running external programs or moving to certain slides.
You can also decide how your button appears on a slide.

The process of adding an action button to a slide involves first
creating the button itself, then defining its function.

Add a button to a slide by following these steps:

1. Click the Slide view button and move to the slide where you
want to add a button.

2. From the Drawing toolbar, click the AutoShapes button and
then click Action Buttons to bring up the Action Buttons
toolbox.

3. In the Action Buttons toolbox, click a button shape. You can
choose buttons that represent actions, such as home, forward,
backward, document, and video. You can embellish the blank
button with text to customize your choices (*see also* Step 6).

4. Click your slide to start drawing the button, starting with the
upper-left corner of the button. Drag the mouse until the
button reaches a size of your satisfaction; then release the
mouse button.

After you complete this step, a dialog box appears and
suggests you save your PowerPoint document before creating
the hyperlink. It is recommended that you name your document and save it before proceeding.

5. In the Action Settings dialog box that appears, assign an
action to your newly created button. Assign the action on
either the Mouse Click or Mouse Over tab. Choosing Mouse
Click requires the presenter to click the button in order to
execute its action, while choosing Mouse Over requires only
that the presenter move the mouse on top of the button
(without clicking) to perform the button action.

Default actions are preset for many buttons, but you may want
to redefine button actions according to your specific needs.
For instance, returning to the home slide (the first slide in the

presentation) is the default action for the action button which looks like a house. Your options in defining the Action Settings for your buttons are as follows:

- **None:** No action is taken.

- **Hyperlink to:** Activates a drop-down list indicating everywhere the jump can go. *See also* "Adding Hyperlinks" in this part.

- **Run program:** Allows you to choose an external program to run when the button is clicked. *Note:* If you choose this option, you need to make certain that the external program is available on whatever system you run your presentation.

- **Run macro:** Produces a list of all available macros in the presentation. *See also* Part X for details on macros.

- **Object action:** Applies to a non-Action Button object to which you attach an action. This option lets you identify what action will be taken when the object is clicked or moused over. For example, you can attach the Play action to a movie object.

- **Play sound:** Plays a sound in conjunction with any other action taken. You can choose from sounds in PowerPoint's Clip Gallery or your own files. A neat idea here is to play a cash register sound when clicking a button that links to an Excel financial spreadsheet. *See also* Part VI for details on sounds.

- **Highlight click:** Applies to a non-Action Button object to which you attach an action. Because Action Buttons highlight when clicked or moused over, checking this option allows other objects — like shapes or text boxes — to look as if they too are being click or moused over.

6. Tweak the button's appearance: Pull the handles to adjust button size, and yank on the diamond handle to alter the 3-D effect of the button. Move the entire button by clicking it and dragging it to another place on your slide. Adjust the fill color as you would for any drawing object (***see also*** Part IV for details).

You can add text to any selected button by right-clicking the action button, choosing Add Text and then typing at the cursor. After text exists, you simply need to click on the text and start typing or editing. Button text can be formatted using the Text formatting toolbar.

Button text looks best on blank buttons.

If you want to change a button's action setting at a later time, right-click the action button and click the Action Settings command.

Adding Hyperlinks

You can format a text object, a single word, or a phrase of text to be a hyperlink to just about anywhere — another slide, another PowerPoint presentation, another program, or even a Web site. Clicking a hyperlink allows you to move dynamically through your slides — not just in boring linear order.

Follow these steps to create a hyperlink:

1. Click to select a text object that you want to designate as a hyperlink. You can also select a single word or other short phrase of text by highlighting the text.

2. To bring up the Insert Hyperlink dialog box, click the Insert Hyperlink button on the Standard toolbar or choose Insert⇨Hyperlink.

3. To link to a file or a Web site, type the filename or URL in the Link to file or URL text box. To locate a file, click the top Browse button, make a selection, and click OK.

To link to another slide in the current presentation, click the Name location in file Browse button, make a selection, and click OK.

Note: Check the box labeled Use Relative Path for Hyperlink if you plan on moving the location of the file or destination to which you are hyperlinking. Checking this box sets up the hyperlink without regard to the absolute location of the file.

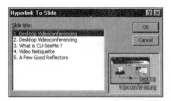

4. Click OK to complete the creation of the hyperlink. Newly created text hyperlinks are highlighted in colors which coordinate with other text on your slide.

Hyperlinks become active only when you're working in Slide Show view. So how can you be sure you created a hyperlink? Regardless of view, the mouse pointer changes to a hand whenever you near a hyperlink. That's how!

To delete a hyperlink:

1. In Slide view, click the hyperlink that you want to remove.

Action button (links to title slide)   Text hyperlink (links to web site)

Desktop Videoconferencing

What is CU-SeeMe ?

http://cu-seeme.cornell.edu/

Video Netiquette

A Few Good Reflectors

Text hyperlink (links to another PowerPoint slide)

 2. Click the Insert Hyperlink button on the Standard toolbar. This step may seem illogical, but the Insert Hyperlink dialog box now appears with a heretofore-unseen button: Remove Link.

3. Click the Remove Link button and say "Hasta la vista, baby" to your hyperlink.

Showing Your Slides via Computer

Those of you choosing to show your stuff with a computer have the greatest control over the presentation process. PowerPoint lets you select several preferences when delivering your slides, dependent upon whether you'll be presenting them to a formal audience, collaborating on them with colleagues connected over a network, or letting an individual peruse them leisurely at a kiosk.

PowerPoint offers some nifty keyboard and mouse commands that empower you with extra control before your audience. One neat feature is a mouse pen that lets you doodle notes on each slide as you go. You can even pack up the show and play it on computers not loaded with PowerPoint software. The whole process begins with the Set Up Show dialog box.

Choosing presentation styles in the Set Up Show dialog box

After you finish creating your individual slides and testing out your cool animation, summon the Set Up dialog box, where you make some final decisions about how your show will be presented.

Choose Slide Show⇨Set Up Show and then mark your choices as follows in the Set Up Show dialog box:

✦ **Show type:** Click one of the three radio buttons at the top to select whether the show will be presented by a speaker (that's you!), browsed by an individual, or browsed at a kiosk. (You can choose only one of these options.)

• Clicking Presented by a speaker sets up a full-screen presentation in which a speaker controls how the show is presented — including taking meeting minutes and recording actions items.

• Browsed by an individual sets up a smaller screen presentation, which appears in its own window with commands available for navigating the show, and for editing and printing slides. Other files can be open on-screen at the same time. This option is most frequently used by someone who browses the show over a company intranet.

• Clicking Browsed at a kiosk creates a self-running presentation which is most often used at an unattended display at a convention or a mall. Navigation commands can be included to give users perusing the show control over which slides they choose to see.

Next, click one or more of the three check boxes at the top to choose whether the show should

• Loop continuously (start over at the first slide after the show finishes) until the presenter or user presses the Esc key

• Show without narrations (which may have been recorded at the Slide Show menu)

• Show without animations (which shows slides in their final forms as if all animations have been performed)

If you previously selected Browsed by an individual, you can also check the Show Scrollbar box. This option places a scrollbar on the slide show window to make all parts of the window accessible to the person viewing the show.

✦ **Slides:** Choose to show All the slides in the presentation or
specify a range in the From and To boxes. You may also
choose to present a Custom Show you have created from your
presentation. Click the tab to reveal a drop-down box of
Custom Shows available. The Custom Show tab is deselected
if you have no Custom Shows. *See also* "Creating Custom
Shows" later in this section for more information.

✦ **Advance slides:** Choose whether the presenter or user
manually proceeds from slide to slide or whether the slides
should advance according to timings that you've set. *See also*
"Automating the slide show with slide timings" later in this
section.

✦ **Pen color:** Accept the default color for the pen tool, or get a
little crazy and change to some other color. *See also* "Writing
with the slide show pen" later in this section.

It's a good idea to always choose the Loop continuously until Esc
option. That way, when you complete your presentation, you
return to your first slide. Without looping back, your audience will
end up staring at ugly old Slide Sorter view when you click off your
final slide.

Writing with the slide show pen

The slide show pen is a handy resource for pointing out key text or
important items on a slide during your presentation. It serves the
same purpose as a laser pointer, except that the marks created by
the pen stay on the slide until another slide is transitioned to
during the slide show.

Notes are not permanent! If you leave a slide and then return, the notes will have vanished. So don't write anything important with the pen.

Here are a couple points you should keep in mind:

✦ You can summon the pen during a show by right-clicking the mouse and pointing to Pen in the menu. Write on the slide by clicking and holding the left mouse button while simultaneously moving the mouse as you would a writing utensil. After writing on a slide, you need to right-click and switch back to the Arrow so that you can continue navigating your presentation.

✦ You can also hide the slide show pen or pointer during a slide show. To hide the pen or pointer, right-click the mouse, select Pointer Options, and click Hide Now or Hide Always:

• **Hide Now** turns off the pen or pointer temporarily. As soon as you move the mouse, the pen or pointer reappears.

• **Hide Always** turns off the pen or pointer for the remainder of the slide show.

The writing color of the pen is preset to coordinate with the color scheme of your slides, but this color can be changed at any time to suit your own personal taste.

To change pen color prior to starting a slide show, select Slide Show⇨Set Up Show from the menu bar. Click your choice of color in the Pen Color box. To change pen color during a slide show, right-click the mouse, select Pointer Options⇨Pen Color and pick a new color.

Presenting slide shows manually

If you choose to run the show manually (see the preceding section for your other options), start by moving to the first slide in your presentation. Then initiate the slide show by choosing Slide Show⇨View Show or by clicking the Slide Show view button from the view buttons in the lower-left corner.

Besides speaking eloquently and making eye contact with your audience members, you'll spend the majority of time delivering a manually-run PowerPoint slide show performing the following tasks:

✦ **Moving along:** The first slide of your show appears and stays on-screen until you click the left mouse button.

If you created animation that builds your slide one bullet at a time, only the unanimated objects appear at the start of each slide. Click the mouse button to show the first animation and continue clicking to advance each additional animation in turn. When all animations on a slide are completed, click the mouse button to transition to the next slide.

✦ **Writing notes:** Make notes on a slide by picking up the pen and then holding down the left mouse button as you draw. Release the button to stop drawing.

Use the following shortcuts to perform any of these other slick presentation tasks.

To Do This	Perform This Action
Show Actions menu	Right-click
Advance to next animation or next slide	Left-click, press spacebar, press forward arrow, or press down arrow
Back up one animation or slide	Press Backspace back arrow, or up arrow
Show specific slide	Press slide number and then press Enter
Toggle screen black	Press B
Toggle screen white	Press W
Show/hide pointer	Press A or =
Change arrow to pen	Press Ctrl+P
Change pen to arrow	Press Ctrl+A
Erase screen doodles	Press E
End slide show	Press Esc

You can use a whole bunch of other shortcuts, but just be aware that a handful of other keyboard sequences will yield certain bizarre results during your slide show. Don't get too curious about what those may be during a really important presentation to the board of directors.

Automating the slide show with slide timings

Use slide timings whenever you want to create a stand-alone show. This option allows you to designate how long each slide appears on-screen before advancing to the next slide.

To set the slide timings:

1. Choose Slide Show⇨Rehearse Timings from the menu bar. A small Rehearsal dialog box with a timer appears in the corner of the screen.

The Rehearsal dialog box times how long each slide is displayed, as well as the total time for the entire presentation. Both times are displayed in the dialog box.

2. Display each slide for whatever duration you choose; advance to the next slide by left-clicking, pressing the spacebar, or pressing the forward arrow button in the Rehearsal dialog box. PowerPoint records how long each slide is presented.

If you screw up timing a slide, click the Repeat button and try timing the slide again.

3. After the last slide is timed, PowerPoint informs you of the total time for the show and asks whether you want to record the presentation as timed. Click Yes to accept your timings or No to ditch them.

Run the timed show by clicking the Using Timings if Present radio button in the Set Up Show dialog box. (***See also*** "Choosing presentation styles in the Set Up Show dialog box" earlier in this part.) And then go play hooky while PowerPoint does all the work!

Creating Custom Shows

PowerPoint Custom Shows allow you to create multiple, customized presentations from a single slide show. Instead of building entirely separate — but similar — presentations for unique audience groupings, PowerPoint lets you pick a subset of slides from your presentation and bundle them together as a Custom Show. You can even create multiple Custom Shows from a single presentation.

For instance, you can create a 20-slide presentation for an employee briefing, and then customize a 10-slide executive summary subset of the briefing for top-level managers. You could then create a 15-slide Custom Show from the same material for a different audience.

After developing a Custom Show, you can edit it by adding or deleting slides at any time.

To create a custom slide show:

1. Select Slide Show⇨Custom Shows from the menu bar.

2. At the Custom Shows dialog box, click New.

The Define Custom Show dialog box appears.

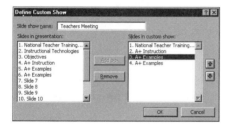

3. In the Slide show name box, type a name for your Custom Show.

4. In the Slides in presentation box, click a slide you want to add to your Custom Show, and press Add. Repeat for each slide you want added.

Added slides appear in the Slides in Custom Show box.

5. To reorder slides in the Custom Show, click a slide in the Slides in Custom Show box that you wish to move. Press the up or down arrow in the Define Custom Shows dialog box to move the selected slide up or down in the presentation order.

6. Click OK to accept your Custom Show.

This returns you to the Custom Shows dialog box.

7. Press Close to exit the dialog box.

You can preview your Custom Show, by clicking the name of the show in the Custom Shows dialog box, and clicking the Show button.

Editing a Custom Show

A Custom Show can be edited after it has been created. Add or
delete slides from a Custom Show as follows:

1. Select Slide Show⇨Custom Shows from the menu bar.

2. At the Custom Shows dialog box, click the name of the Custom
Show you want to edit, and press Edit.

The Define Custom Shows dialog box opens.

3. To add a slide to your Custom Show: In the Slides in presentation box, click a slide you want to add to your Custom Show,
and press Add. Repeat for each slide you want added. Added
slides appear in the Slides in Custom Show box.

4. To delete a slide from your Custom Show: In the Slides in
Custom Show box, click a slide you want to remove from your
Custom Show, and click Remove. Removed Slides return to the
Slides in presentation box.

5. To reorder slides in the Custom Show, click a slide in the
Slides in Custom Show box that you wish to move. Press the
up or down arrow in the Define Custom Shows dialog box to
move the selected slide up or down in the presentation order.

6. Click OK to accept your Custom Show.

This returns you to the Custom Shows dialog box.

7. Press Close to exit the dialog box.

To delete an entire Custom Show, click its name in the Custom
Shows dialog box, and press Remove. Only the Custom Show itself
is removed — not the original slides of the presentation.

Presenting over a network

Why make everyone drive — or even walk to another building —
when you can conduct your meetings via computer network?
PowerPoint 97 offers you a cool new feature to help make each of
those virtual meetings a success: It lets you present a complete
slide show that appears on all participants' computers, right at
their very own desks. Participants can even use the drawing pen
to doodle and make notes as you go. The only hitch is that
everyone must have PowerPoint 97 installed.

To show a presentation over a network:

1. Open the presentation.

2. Choose Tools⇨Presentation Conference from the menu bar.

3. When asked by PowerPoint, provide the network name of each computer that will join the conference.

Your colleagues need only start PowerPoint 97 at their own computers, and choose Tools➪Presentation Conference from the menu bar. It's up to you to start the show! You may also want to use audioconferencing, either over the Internet or by plain ol' telephone, to speak to your audience as you show the slides.

Presenting without PowerPoint installed: The Pack and Go Wizard

In case you have to give a show without your trusty computer, you'll want to avoid the possibility (and embarrassment!) of reaching your final destination and discovering that PowerPoint isn't installed at the other end. You can't legally copy PowerPoint onto the destination computer — and you wouldn't want to go through the lengthy install process anyway. Your best bet is to use PowerPoint's Pack and Go feature.

Pack and Go neatly bundles your presentation, presentation fonts, and a PowerPoint viewer onto a diskette. You can then pop this diskette into the destination computer and present your slide show — even though the computer has no PowerPoint!

A simple Wizard guides you through the packaging process:

1. Open the PowerPoint presentation that you want to pack and go.

2. Choose File➪Pack and Go from the Menu bar.

3. Follow the wizard screens to completion, inserting a destination disk when prompted.

Some notes on packaging with the wizard:

✦ Be sure to package the Active presentation.

✦ The wizard asks which drive you want your packaged presentation sent to. If your slide show is short and mainly composed of text, you'll probably be able to fit the whole thing on a floppy disk (most likely your drive A). However, if your slide show is large or uses lots of pictures, video, or sound, you may have to store its package on a Zip or Jaz disk (most likely your drive F or G).

✦ Click to place a check in the Include linked files and Embed TrueType fonts checkboxes. Clicking the linked files option causes sounds and videos that your slides call upon to be included in your presentation. Clicking the fonts option helps ensure that your presentation will show text in the same fonts from which is was originally constructed — even if the destination computer doesn't have those fonts installed.

✦ Be sure to include the PowerPoint Viewer with your packaged file. This is the little program which makes it possible to play your presentation on computers where PowerPoint is not installed.

Check whether you'll be using a Macintosh or a Windows system at your destination. Remember that PowerPoint 97 is currently supported only on the Windows platform. If you know you'll be using a Mac, you need to save your presentation as PowerPoint 4.0 and beg the owners of your destination computer to install a Mac PowerPoint 4.0 Viewer on the system. (Good luck.)

To run the packaged presentation on a destination computer:

1. Insert the disk containing the packaged program into the drive of the destination computer.

2. Click the Start button, click Run, and browse to locate the Pngsetup.exe program from the disk. Click OK to run the program.

3. Double-click the PowerPoint Viewer icon created by the setup program. The PowerPoint Viewer dialog box appears.

4. Click the presentation that you want to show. A thumbnail of the selected presentation appears in the dialog box.

5. Click Show to start the presentation.

All keyboard and mouse shortcuts are activated, just as they operate on your native system.

Showing Your Slides via Other Resources

The ultimate goal of creating your slides is, of course, to show them. PowerPoint is at its best when shown on a computer, but the masters of Microsoft recognize that not everyone can command this presentation format. Consequently, PowerPoint offers you a handful of nifty viewing options by which you can display your presentation to your audience.

High-tech and medium-tech options employ the computer and offer flexibility in the way you present your slides. Low-tech options, however, require no computer but somewhat limit you in the methods you use to display slides.

High-tech options

A great way to present your PowerPoint slides to large audiences is through a big-screen television. By using a scan converter to synchronize the computer output and the television signals, you can display a crisp replica of your computer-generated slides on the television screen.

Running your computer output through a scan converter is also the option of choice for those of you planning to display your slides via closed-circuit TV, satellite, or compressed video. This option can range from very cheap to very expensive. Be prepared to spend $100 for a low-end scan converter and $2,000 for a spectacular one. Don't forget to consider also the costs associated with purchasing televisions (regular or big screen) for the viewing audiences at each of your receive sites.

Medium-tech options

Another option for showing slides is to run the computer output through a projector that beams onto a white screen. Such projectors also maintain fairly crisp images when reproducing your slides several feet high in proportion. The downside to these projection systems is that they are often pricey — they can easily cost several thousand dollars.

Another medium-tech option is to send the computer output to an *LCD* panel — a liquid crystal display panel. The LCD panel is a lightweight, portable screen that sits atop an overhead projector. When the overhead is turned on, it projects the computer images of the LCD panel onto a white screen. The clarity of the LCD is not nearly as sharp, however, as other display options.

Low-tech options

For instances where you simply have no means of showing your slides through a computer, PowerPoint provides you two low-tech presentation options: overhead transparencies and 35mm slides. *See also* Part VII.

Part IX

Publishing the Presentation

It's a good idea to make your presentation longer-lived than the single hour you spend soliloquizing and mouse-clicking PowerPoint slides. Audience members are likely to want to jot down notes as you speak, and you'll come off as the consummate professional by providing them a take-home printout of slides used in your presentation. You'll also find that PowerPoint ensures your success with multiple presentation options — including computerless formats like 35mm slides and transparencies — just in case you find yourself operating in a technology-free zone. Lastly, for those of you wishing to publish your presentation for a worldwide audience, I show you a quick and easy way to post your PowerPoint slide show on the web.

In this part . . .

✔ **Printing handouts of PowerPoint slides**

✔ **Adding speaker notes to your slides**

✔ **Presenting with 35mm slides and transparencies**

✔ **Publishing PowerPoint slides on the web**

Attaching Notes to a Slide

Notes are like little speaker cue cards, perfect for reminding you to tell a joke, make eye contact, or pause contemplatively. I use them frequently for elaborating at great length on the cursory bullet items I use onscreen. Notes don't appear during the slide show presentation itself, only in slide construction mode. But they can be printed out and hidden at the podium for your use during the real deal.

Trying the Notes Page view

One note page exists for every slide in your presentation. Pressing the Notes Page View button calls up an extended page in which your slide appears at the top and the notes appear at the bottom.

You can switch to Notes Page view in two ways:

❖ Click the Notes Page view button.

❖ Select View⇨Notes Page.

Typing notes

Add notes to any slide in your presentation as follows:

1. Move to the slide where you want to add speaker notes.

2. Click on the Notes Page view button to change to Notes Page view.

3. Click the Notes text box and begin typing.

The text box allows you to type and format text in the same fashion you would in any word-processing document. You can change text fonts, sizes, and colors and add bullets or numbers to help you format. Remember, these notes are for you; perfect spelling and font size are more important on the slide itself — not the notes.

Making room for more notes

Just in case you're the wordy type and you run out of room for your notes, you have three options for increasing notes space:

❖ **Increase the size of your Notes text box:** Grab a handle at the top of the text box and stretch upwards to resize the box. You'll probably need to shrink the size of the thumbnail of the slide: Click the slide, grab a handle, and resize as needed to make room for the expanding text box. This change impacts only the current page. If you want to increase the size of the notes text box for all the pages, you need to make adjustments to the Notes Master. ***See also*** Part III for details on editing the Notes Master.

✦ **Add another notes page:** This feature allows you to include significantly more notes than can be typed on a single page. To add another notes page:

1. Press New Slide from the Common Tasks Toolbar or press Ctrl+M to insert a new slide immediately following the slide in need of more notes. It doesn't matter which format you choose in the AutoLayout dialog box.

2. On the newly inserted slide, click the Notes Page view button to change to Notes Page view.

3. Click on the slide thumbnail and press delete or Ctrl+X.

4. Click the notes text box and drag the handles to resize until this box occupies most of the page.

5. Continue typing your extra notes in the notes text box of this new slide.

6. Click the Hide Slide button or select Slide Show⎸Hide Slide to prevent the dummy slide from appearing in the Slide Show.

✦ **Delete the slide placeholder:** If you're a real space hog, you can just click and delete the slide placeholder at the top of the notes page. This doesn't delete the slide itself — just its placeholder on the notes page.

Getting Ready to Print

As in other Microsoft Office programs, the easiest way to print your PowerPoint slides is to click the Print button on the Standard toolbar. This button does not bring up any choices or options — it simply prints a single copy of your entire presentation.

 To see more options for printing your presentation, open the Print dialog box. Open the Print dialog box using one of these methods:

✦ Choose File⇨Print from the menu bar.

✦ Press Ctrl+P.

✦ Press Ctrl+Shift+F12.

Choosing OK in the Print dialog box without changing any options has the same effect as simply clicking the Print button on the Standard toolbar. However, tweaking the options in the dialog box provides much greater flexibility in the way you execute the print job.

The Print dialog box offers the option of changing any of these parameters:

✦ The printer on which your PowerPoint presentation is printed

✦ Which slides are printed

✦ The number of copies printed

✦ What is printed, from slides only to slides with speaker notes

✦ How many slides are printed on a page

✦ Whether slides are printed in color, grayscale, or black and white

The Print dialog box does not, however, arrange to load paper when the printer's paper tray runs out.

Changing printers

Use the Printer name drop-down menu to select which printer spits out your document. Available printers — including an option to fax — are listed in the Name field when you click the arrow tab. If you don't see the name of a printer to which you're networked, you need to install that printer's driver before you can use it for a print job.

After you select a printer, click the Properties button to adjust printing properties such as paper size, source tray, graphics resolutions, and page orientation (portrait or landscape). The properties available depend on the printer you are using.

Selecting a print range

One of the nifty little attributes of the Print dialog box is the flexibility it affords in printing out your PowerPoint presentation. If you find a ghastly mistake on a single slide, you don't have to reprint every slide all over again; you can simply print the part of the presentation you messed up the first time. The Print Range portion gives you the following options when printing your slides:

+ **All:** Prints the whole shebang — every slide — from start to finish.

+ **Current slide:** Prints just the slide you're on.

+ **Selection:** Prints only the slides in the range you've already selected. This option is available only after you highlight slides for printing from the Outline or Slide Sorter views. The advantage? It permits you to print your range without having to remember slide numbers.

+ **Custom Show:** Prints a custom show you've previously saved.

+ **Slides:** Prints only specific slide numbers and slide ranges of the entire presentation. For instance, if you reorder slides 2, 3, and 4, and then find spelling errors on slides 9 and 11, you type 2-4,9,11. Only slides 2, 3, 4, 9, and 11 will be reprinted.

Selecting the number of copies

The Copies area of the Print dialog box is where you get to think like a photocopier. Use the Number of copies spinner to choose how many copies you want, and click the spinner until your chosen number appears in the box. Also click a radio button to indicate whether you want to collate copies or keep copies of the same sheet bundled together. You may want to consider sparing your ink cartridge by printing only one copy and then using a real photocopier to do the grunt work of mass duplication.

Specifying what you want printed

The Print What pulldown menu at the bottom of the Print dialog box lets you make a few choices to specify exactly what you want to print.

Here are your options:

+ **Slides:** Prints individual slides, one per page. This option is available only when your slides are animation-free.

✦ **Slides (with animations):** Prints individual slides, one per page, adding one new animation event per page. Prints each slide as it appears at the completion of each animation. Think hard about whether you really need to print this level of separation and detail, as it takes up reams and reams of paper.

✦ **Slides (without animations):** Prints individual slides, one per page, as if all animation events on a slide have been completed. Also shows animation images and text which may exist onscreen only briefly during the slide show (such as animations with the flash effect).

✦ **Notes pages:** Prints each slide, one per page, as a small thumbnail followed by a text box full of speaker notes. *See also* "Printing Notes Pages" in this part.

✦ **Handouts:** Includes the option of printing two, three, or six slides per page for distribution to audience members who wish to forever treasure your memorable presentation. *See also* "Printing Audience Handouts" in this part.

✦ **Outline view:** Prints an ordered, text-only outline version of your slides from start to finish. Saves space when you require a printout only of what is said, not how it looks.

Choosing more options

The remaining check boxes residing at the bottom of the Print dialog box perform a handful of important functions. Here's what they do:

✦ **Print hidden slides:** Includes images of hidden slides in your handouts, even if you don't show them in your slide show. This option is useful for providing audience participants with additional reference information that may be too elementary, too advanced, or too time-consuming to include in your formal presentation. *See also* "Printing Notes Pages."

✦ **Scale to fit paper:** Checks the size of the paper in the printer and adjusts the size of the printing accordingly.

✦ **Black & white:** Select this option only if you have a black and white printer, as the printer will attempt to produce colors as shades of gray.

✦ **Pure black & white:** Prints dark grays and blacks as black and prints light grays and whites as white. Works well for text only.

✦ **Frame slides:** Draws a pretty little black picture frame around each slide on the printout.

Printing Audience Handouts

Audiences are often grateful for copies of slides you present during your presentation — not to mention that you may look more organized and professional. The appearance of audience handouts depends on how many slides you want to cram onto a page — and subsequently how large you want each printed slide to appear. You have the option of printing two, three, or six slides per page.

 The three per page option offers a nice mix of adequate slide size and empty space for participants to jot down their own notes. But if you're a tree-hugger, go for the six per page option and duplex your handouts front and back.

Print audience handouts as follows:

1. Open the Print Dialog Box using File⇨Print.

2. Using the Print what drop-down list, select Handouts with two, three, or six slides per page.

3. Click OK to start printing.

Printing Speaker Notes

Notes pages can be printed just for the speaker or — if you think they're really compelling — for audience members attending your presentation. Such notes can be particularly useful for audiences listening to detailed or complex information: Having your notes pages in hand allows them to focus their attention on your presentation without struggling to scrawl your comments at the same time.

Notes pages with blank notes textboxes also can be useful for people attending your presentation because they give attendees handy sheets for jotting down their own thoughts during your presentation.

Print notes pages as follows:

1. Open the Print Dialog Box using File⇨Print.

2. In the Print what box, select Notes Pages.

3. Check Print hidden slides if you've created slides with extra notes pages.

4. Click OK to start printing.

Printing Transparencies

If you choose to print transparencies, you should execute the following steps at the time you build your new presentation. If you have already built a presentation and then decide to produce it as a set of transparencies, perform these same steps prior to stuffing the little sheets of plastic into your printer.

1. Choose File⇨Page Setup to call up the Page Setup dialog box. If you are retrofitting an existing presentation for output as transparencies, be aware that you need to examine how this retrofit affects each of your slides. You may need to move or resize slide elements to better fit them to their new printed size and page orientation. If you are building a new presentation, don't worry about retrofitting.

2. Choose Overhead from the Slides sized for menu.

3. In the Orientation section, choose Slides and select the Portrait option.

You should also consider using a relatively stark white background, limiting the use of elaborate graphics, and avoiding color unless you have access to a color printer. Also think about running a paper copy of your slides before you print them to transparency sheets — making an error on paper is much cheaper than making it on plastic!

Be sure to check whether your printer has the capability of printing directly onto transparencies. Those that don't may melt or otherwise degrade while printing is in progress! Even if your printer is capable of printing transparencies, you need to make sure you pick transparency sheets that are designed for your type of printer. You also need to check which side of the transparency sheet is designated as the print surface. Printing on the wrong side of the sheet can result in poor image quality because the ink fails to properly bond with the plastic.

Printing 35mm Slides

PowerPoint slides can be converted for use in a 35mm slide carousel with a little extra effort. You'll need to ensure that slide dimensions are sized for 35mm and then take your final presentation to a special facility that churns out the little guys.

To set up your slides for 35mm printing, follow these steps:

1. When you create a new PowerPoint file, choose File⇨Page Setup to open the Page Setup dialog box.

2. Choose 35mm Slides from the Slides sized for menu.

3. In the Orientation section, choose Slides and select the Landscape option.

At your neighborhood photo lab

Take a disk file of your slide presentation to your local photo processing center. You may want to check whether they use Mac or Windows so you know how to format your disk. Remember to embed True Type fonts so that your text prints out the same on the physical slides as it looks onscreen. Since printing 35mm slides tends to be a bit pricey (around $10 per slide), you won't want to print up too many. So avoid including animations, and for goodness sakes, avoid spelling errors!

Via Genigraphics

Genigraphics is a company that will create 35mm slides for you. All you have to do is send your them your presentation on disk or online, and if you plan ahead you can get your slides for as little as $7 each. You can charge the work to a major credit card or have them bill you. They'll even do large color posters, spiral-bound presentation booklets, and banners on the Goodyear blimp. Okay, so they won't do blimps.

Here's how to use their services:

1. Choose File⇨Send To⇨Genigraphics. This action invokes a Genigraphics wizard that leads you through the rest of the process.

2. At the Genigraphics wizard welcome screen, click Next. Check the 35mm Slides output box or check another box that indicates your output preference.

3. Click Next and indicate what presentation you want to send and how you want to send it. Genigraphics gives you the option of sending via modem, through the Internet, or on disk.

4. Click Next and continue to complete the questions the wizard asks. You need to decide on the type of slide mounts (plastic or glass), the shipping method, the ship-to location, the turnaround time (faster is more expensive), and the payment method.

> *Note:* You need to complete two very important check boxes. One involves whether you want to print hidden slides — why would you? The other asks whether you want to print animation builds or not. With the exception of a slide that builds only the most critical point of your presentation, I wouldn't spend the money to print every build of every slide. That's a quick way to turn a $7 slide into a $28 set of 4 slides — it's not worth it.

5. Continue clicking Next until you have completed all the questions.

6. Click Finish. At this point, your modem will deliver the order or you'll need to mail off the disk.

Publishing on the Web

One way you may want to publish your PowerPoint presentation is on the World Wide Web. People in attendance at your presentation can share your content with others by encouraging them to go online and click through your slide show with Netscape Navigator or Internet Explorer.

Absent personnel have no excuses for missing your message because they can at least glean key points from the web show. You can also give your presentation some longevity and added accessibility by posting it on the web.

PowerPoint 97 offers a quick and easy option for translating your slide shows into the HTML language required for publishing web pages online.

You don't need to know how to write HTML code to put your PowerPoint slide show on the web. All you need to know is how to follow the lead of yet another wizard.

Converting to HTML with the wizard

Pace yourself, and follow these steps as the Save as HTML wizard helps you decide how to set up your web presentation:

1. Invoke the Save as HTML wizard by selecting File⇨Save as HTML from the main menu.

2. The Save as HTML wizard appears. Click <u>N</u>ext.

3. Choose to convert your PowerPoint slides to the web with a N<u>e</u>w layout or choose to <u>L</u>oad existing layout. Click <u>N</u>ext.

The <u>L</u>oad existing layout option will be highlighted only when you have saved the settings of previous slide conversions to the web. Selecting this option lets you bypass much of the wizard.

4. Choose between the <u>S</u>tandard web page format and the B<u>r</u>owser frames format. Click <u>N</u>ext.

- **Standard:** Slides are shown individually, and they comprise the main field of the browser area. Users navigate the slides by using a panel of buttons.

- **Browser frames:** Divides the browser screen into separate frames. Only one frame shows the PowerPoint slides. Other frames show navigation buttons, outline notes, and information from the notes pages.

WYSIWYG (what you see is what you get) does not apply to browser frames — users may get a lot of unexpected junk, depending on how you constructed your original PowerPoint slides. For instance, if you created slides without typing slide titles in their designated placeholders, those titles will not appear in the frame containing the outline of your presentation. It's a good idea to preview your converted presentation before posting it online for all the world to see.

5. Choose the format of your graphics files by clicking the associated radio button. Click <u>N</u>ext. The wizard will ultimately convert your slides to graphics files for the web. Here's how your file format choices differ:

- **GIF:** An uncompressed file format frequently used for web graphics.

- **JPEG:** A compressible format that allows you to reduce the file size of the graphics you post to the web. Compression also reduces image quality, but it improves the speed at which users can load and view your presentation.

  Note: If you want your users to be able to view your presentation in nearly its native format, you need to use PowerPoint Animation. This special PowerPoint format allows animations such as flying bullets to play in the web browser as if the presentation is actually being played in PowerPoint. The PowerPoint Animation viewer is automatically downloaded and installed to the user's system at the first playing of a slide show on the web.

6. Select the monitor resolution of the displays on which you expect the presentation to be viewed, along with the <u>W</u>idth of graphics. Click <u>N</u>ext.

Most web aficionados can display at least 800 by 600. The Width of graphics option allows you to have slides occupy ¹/₄, ¹/₂, or ³/₄ the width of the destination screen.

7. Type in the text boxes to provide the text you want to appear on the web information page. Click Download original presentation if you want users to be able to retrieve the original PowerPoint slide show. Click Next.

The web information page is the page preceding the pages that show your slides. You can provide your Email address, Your home page address, and any Other information you want displayed there.

8. Choose between the Use browser colors option and the Custom Colors option to select the web page color and button look. Click Next.

Use browser colors displays your web information page and the background behind your slides using colors preset by each user's web browser. Custom colors allows you to decide how everything will look on the user's display. If you select Custom colors you will be given additional options for choosing attributes about how the background color, text, links, and visited links will appear. You will also be offered the option of making navigation buttons transparent. The Custom colors option displays a palette so that you can view your color choice selections as you make them.

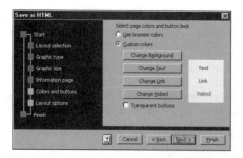

9. Select a button style for users to navigate your slides. Click Next.

10. Check whether to Include slide notes in pages. Click Next. If you selected the Standard web page layout, this screen will also ask you to choose where you want navigation buttons placed onscreen.

11. Indicate where you want the folder containing the HTML files to be located. Click Next. The HTML files will be contained within a single folder. It's a good idea to locate this folder with other PowerPoint files you archive on your computer. However, because the files sometimes occupy several megabytes of memory, you may instead choose to save them on a zip disk or other external storage device.

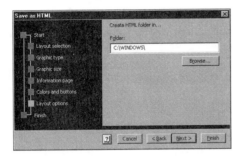

12. Click Finish.

13. Type a name if you want to save the settings you've defined in the Save as HTML wizard. Click Save. If you don't want to keep the settings, press Don't Save.

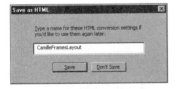

14. The wizard informs you of its progress as it converts each slide to HTML. When the conversion is complete, click OK.

Viewing your presentation as HTML

To preview how your converted presentation will appear on the web, you need to examine the contents of the HTML folder the wizard creates. The folder contains a long list of files that make sense only when viewed through a trusty web browser like Netscape Navigator or Internet Explorer.

Here's the process for checking out your newly created HTML:

1. Locate the folder containing the HTML files of your PowerPoint presentation. The folder has the same name as the presentation, and is stored according to your specifications in the Convert to HTML Wizard.

2. Double-click on the folder containing your HTML files.

3. Look through the contents of the file and double-click on the file labeled index.html. This file may alternatively be titled just index.

4. Watch as your default web browser boots and displays the introduction web page.

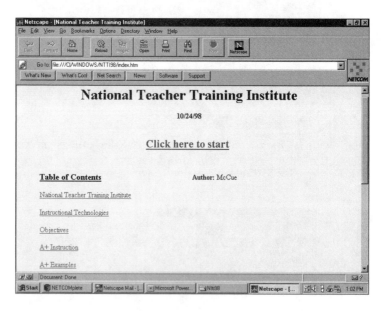

5. Use the navigation buttons accompanying your web slide presentation to move forward and backward through the slides.

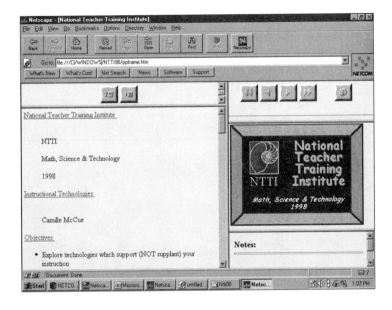

Publishing your presentation online

In order for other lucky web surfers to share in the joy of your PowerPoint slide show, you need to upload the complete HTML folder to a web server. Your company may be able to accomplish this feat in-house, or you may instead choose to call a local web service provider for recommendations on web site hosting.

Changing information in your basic PowerPoint presentation is an easy task, but changing stuff once the presentation is online requires significantly more labor. Some web hosting services charge a fee every time you make a change. Check and double-check your HTML slides (especially spelling!) before you send them off for online posting.

After your presentation has finally made its home on the web, prod a few willing colleagues into going online and trying out your presentation. If they give feedback like "screens are slow to load," you may want to redo your HTML conversion with JPEG graphics at a greater compression. After all, you want users to stay awhile once they've come to visit! *See also* "Converting to HTML with the wizard" in this part for more information on graphics choices.

Part X

Tips, Tricks, and Troubleshooting

For all the other important items that didn't fit clearly in other chapters, I bequeath to you this grab bag. Consider it your five-and-dime store of PowerPoint. Here you can find creative goodies, including slide show ideas which make the most of PowerPoint's prowess. You can also find general computer advice — like managing unwieldy hordes of slide show files — that a good PowerPoint user like yourself is wise to follow. Most importantly, I share with you therapeutic ways of dealing with Murphy's Law disasters, which inevitably plague even the most innocuous PowerPoint user.

In this part . . .

- ✔ Creating creative slide shows
- ✔ Managing PowerPoint files
- ✔ Moving around quickly with keystroke shortcuts
- ✔ Combining multiple actions in one macro button
- ✔ Controlling damage when problems occur

Creative Slide Show Ideas

PowerPoint is known as *the* effective presentation tool, but you may not know the full extent of its capabilities. Here are a few presentation ideas I've used — and observed others using — that you may find work well for you.

For business

Do you want to show employees your new organizational infra-structure? Convey a new corporate strategy to stockholders at your annual meeting? Motivate management to deal with issues of low morale? Then try out some of the following PowerPoint presentation concepts for conveying key messages in business-related situations.

+ **Organizational charts:** Show who is moving up the corporate ladder and who is moving down. Use org charts to explain the chain of command, who reports to whom, and how divisions interact with one another.

+ **Progress graphs:** Compare growth or decline of sales or services. Express trends over time with line graphs or market share with pie graphs.

+ **Product updates:** Use PowerPoint's capability to blend graphics and text by importing scanned images of new products with bulleted text explaining product specs and market positioning.

+ **Quick Web presence:** Reach a planetful of potential business clients by making important PowerPoint presentations available via online access. Why lose a sales opportunity just because a potential customer can't attend your company's gala product unveiling in person?

+ **Motivational addresses:** Managers need to prod even the best workers out of complacency now and then. Blending imported cartoons, newspaper headlines, famous quotes, and humor-ous video clips can help you create dynamic and inspiring attitude-enhancers.

+ **New employee orientation:** Create an informative presenta-tion to assist new employees in transitioning to your company's way of doing business. Generate orientation handbooks by printing out notes-enhanced slides.

+ **Training classes:** Keep employees up-to-date on new products and procedures with crisp, well-organized slide show presentations.

✦ **Stockholder meetings:** Inform investors of the bottom line with a PowerPoint-enhanced presentation. Include organizational charts, graphs, and imported spreadsheets to convey company activity.

✦ **Business plans:** Generate a well-organized presentation explaining plans for future business ventures. Create slides of major points using short-and-sweet text . . . but use buttons to link to hidden pages of the details, just in case the big boss asks.

✦ **Conventions:** Use PowerPoint's automatic slide show mode to create looped, self-running informational presentations. Run the presentation at a kiosk or display located at your company's booth.

For education

Middle school history educators and college physics professors alike find that PowerPoint is a powerful tool for teaching new content in a crisp, organized format. Check out the following ideas for empowering the classroom with PowerPoint:

✦ **Sponge activities:** Find a crazy cartoon or magazine cover that encompasses your topic for the class day. Import it into a PowerPoint slide and delete the caption or headline. Invite students to generate ideas for replacement text.

✦ **Review quizzes:** Avoid the time-consuming task of word processing and photocopying a class quiz: Just create and display a handful of quiz question slides and have students write their answers on notebook paper.

✦ **Class notes:** Instead of writing class notes on the board or overhead — semester after semester, year after year — create your lecture notes in PowerPoint and retain them on disk for the next time you teach the same class!

✦ **Lectures:** Ever notice how students ignore your oral commentary while they furiously scrawl every class note written on the board? Showing class notes, one PowerPoint slide at a time, helps you present lectures at *your* pace — and maintains student focus on the single slide of information at hand.

✦ **Vocabulary terms:** When practicing new vocabulary in English or a foreign language, use PowerPoint to place pictures or analogous words down the left side of a slide and then ask students to call out matching terms from their new vocabulary lists. Animate the correct matches to fly or drive into the right side of the slide.

✦ **Labeling diagrams:** From flowers to earthworms to maps of Civil War battlefields, insert clip art or a picture and then draw lines and text boxes to label key elements of the image. Print out the unlabelled image and distribute as a homework exercise or quiz.

✦ **Faculty meetings:** If you talk for more than five minutes about your latest class project, you know you'll be ignored (even if the principal asked you to address your fellow educators!). Get your point across in the snappiest, fastest way possible using bulleted text and digitized video of your students in action.

✦ **Open houses:** Parents want to see what their offspring are actually accomplishing in your classroom. Wow them with a PowerPoint presentation of your latest undertakings. Include scanned artwork, recorded singalongs, and digital pictures of field trips.

✦ **Student presentations:** If your students have sufficient access to a PowerPoint-outfitted computer, teach them the basics of creating and showing a simple presentation. Then encourage students to present group projects via animated slide shows as an alternative to traditional reports and posterboard displays.

✦ **Biological classifications and family trees:** Sort out kingdoms and species using the hierarchical structure of an org chart. Help students figure out the exact relationship of Oedipus and his mother through an organizational chart's connecting lines and boxes.

✦ **Historical timelines:** Use simple drawing tools such as the double-arrow line and the callout in AutoShape to create a visual representation of the sequence of historical events. Use meaningful clip art images to help students commit the details to memory more easily.

✦ **Seating charts:** Everything has its place, and so do your students. Use the organizational chart function to create rows and columns of boxes (seats) showing student names. Remember to put the head honcho — you! — at the top of the chart (the front of the room).

For social settings

Whenever and wherever crowds gather for a meeting or a festive soiree, PowerPoint can provide the vehicle for delivering the information you want to share. Here's how:

+ **Town hall meetings:** Use bulleted text to keep the neighbors informed of who is in charge and what bill is up for a vote.

+ **Fund-raisers:** Make use of PowerPoint's capability to generate eye-catching graphs to show a comparison between previous years' achievements and your current fund-raising goal.

+ **Public tours:** Show tourists the layout of where they'll be travelling before the big trip. Note key landmarks and points of interest so they'll know what to photograph when they get there.

+ **Genealogy charts:** Alex Haley traced his family roots; now you can do the same and use PowerPoint to show everyone at the next family reunion. Do your research and then make use of the organizational chart function to create your family tree.

+ **Race routes:** Inform crowds of runners and bicyclists where they're headed with a PowerPoint slide show of the race route. Indicate pit stops, refreshment locations, and, of course, the finish line.

+ **Public auctions:** Use PowerPoint slide images projected on a big screen to show folks at the back of the auditorium exactly what that miniature Chinese engraving looks like. Show slide images of items not physically present for viewing, such as houses and land.

Macros

A *macro* is a user-customized shortcut, an opportunity to develop your own time-saving tricks to employ when building your presentation. To create a macro, you perform a series of keystrokes and menu selections and then give your creation a one-touch name. This process is known as *recording a macro.*

For example, I always start each new PowerPoint file by opening the slide master and changing all my title fonts to 36-point bold Arial. To accomplish this task without a macro, I must choose View⇨Slide Master, click the title box, and choose 36-point font, bold, and Arial from the text formatting toolbar. It's a real hassle. But by recording a macro, I can generate a single menu option that performs the entire sequence of steps.

Macros you create are stored in the presentation file, which means that macros are specific to the presentations in which you recorded them — you can't transport them to other presentations.

Recording a macro

Record a macro using the following procedure:

1. Perform a dry run of the sequence you plan to record as a macro.

2. Choose Tools⇨Macro⇨Record New Macro.

The Record Macro dialog box appears with two empty boxes for you to complete: Macro name and Description.

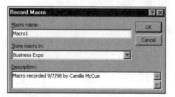

3. Type a name for the macro.

The name cannot contain spaces, commas, or periods. If you do not type a name the macro will be given a default name such as Macro1.

4. Type a description of the macro, indicating what actions it performs.

This step is optional. If you do not type a description, a default phrase will appear indicating who recorded the macro and when it was recorded.

5. Click OK.

 The Record Macro dialog box closes and the Stop Recording toolbar appears in its place.

6. Perform the keystroke and menu sequence that you want the macro to record.

Don't worry if you make a mistake — just stop, return to Step 1 and record again.

7. Click the Stop button to indicate that you're done recording.

The macro is now recorded and is named whatever you called it in the Record Macro dialog box.

Running a macro

Using a previously recorded macro is called *running a macro*. Follow these steps to run a macro:

1. Select Tools⇨Macro⇨Macros.

The Macro dialog box opens and lists all available macros you have recorded.

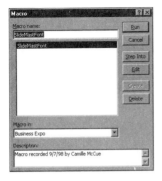

2. Click the macro you want to run.

3. Click <u>R</u>un.

Editing a macro

Editing a macro is a relatively complex task — one that requires you to trudge through lines of code created in a programming language called Visual Basic. Unless you're a glutton for punishment (and you actually enjoy tinkering with computer code), your bet best for editing a macro is to delete the macro and record it again from scratch.

PowerPoint Shortcuts

For tasks you perform repeatedly, several snappy shortcuts are available. Consider committing a handful of your most frequently used tasks to memory — shortcuts can save you a tremendous amount of time in the long run.

Text formatting shortcuts

Press This	*To Change Highlighted Text to This*
Ctrl + B	**Bold**
Ctrl + I	*Italic*
Ctrl + U	<u>Underline</u>
Ctrl + spacebar	Remove all formatting
Ctrl + E	Centered text
Ctrl + L	Left-aligned text
Ctrl + R	Right-aligned text
Ctrl + J	Justified text

Slide master shortcuts

Press This	To Call Up This Master
Shift + 🔲	Slide Master
Shift + ▤	Outline Master
Shift + ▦	Handout Master
Shift + ▣	Notes Master

Other common shortcuts

Pressing This	Performs This Function
Ctrl + X	Cuts highlighted text
Ctrl + C	Copies highlighted text
Ctrl + V	Pastes highlighted text
Ctrl + A	Selects all
Ctrl + N	Creates new document
Ctrl + O	Opens existing document
Ctrl + S	Saves document
Ctrl + P	Prints document
Ctrl + M	Creates new slide

Smart File Management

As a teacher, I'm an inherent pack rat: I save every paper, widget, videotape, and newspaper clipping I may someday want to use to teach a concept. If only I could remember which of my 30-odd boxes I actually stuffed that one particular widget in . . . or if it's really in a box at all.

I strongly recommend organizing and cataloging your PowerPoint projects so that locating and retrieving presentations is a fruitful process. Here are some tips on how to manage PowerPoint files to your best advantage.

Archiving presentations and slides

Save presentations-under-development often, and call them something meaningful. Also consider saving individual slides you tend to use over and over — such as an identification slide with your name, e-mail address, and corporate logo. Just save an individual slide as if it's a really short presentation — a one-slide presentation, to be exact. For more information on saving presentations, *see* Part I.

Maintain consistency in naming files so that you can easily distinguish the contents of one presentation from another without wasting time opening the file. It's best to use a fairly long name which includes the date and terminates with PPT as the filename extension (for instance, `BusExpo8-9.PPT`). However, for files you plan to store on the Internet, avoid using spaces and nonalphabetic symbols in the name.

I find that using folders to logically group like topics together is helpful. You may wish to group by date (months or quarterly cycles) or by subject matter. Be certain to keep call-to files (like movies) in the same folder with the presentation that calls them.

Whatever you do, *don't* store your main PowerPoint files folder in the PowerPoint program folder — keep your content in its own special location, separate from the program files. And remember to keep that special location clutter-free by dumping old, outdated files you don't plan on reusing.

Backing up your work

Most people don't realize the necessity of backing up their work until they experience the agony of losing irreplaceable computer files. Trust me, nothing is worse than working for hours (or days!) to develop a PowerPoint slide show extravaganza, only to have it vanish forever during a freak system failure. So consider backing up like you do buying insurance: Nobody's happy about doing it until tragedy strikes.

The method of backup you choose is entirely up to you. If you have only a handful of critical files, copying everything to a 100MB Zip disk will suffice. But if you have loads and loads of data, you may need to write your files to a recordable CD-ROM or a 1GB (or 2GB) Jaz disk. Another method is to employ Microsoft Backup, a program that performs incremental backup of only the files that have changed that day. Don't feel compelled to rush out and buy Microsoft Backup — you probably already have it because it's a component of Windows 95 and Windows 98. Look for it under Start⇨Programs⇨Accessories⇨System Tools.

You should also back up any files you plan to transport between your home and your office or any other place you plan to access your computer files. When you shuttle files via a notebook computer, consider also making a floppy copy of files — and carrying the floppy separate from the notebook in a nonmagnetic case. If you're really paranoid about losing stuff, you can also send your file as an e-mail attachment from your office account to your home account and vice versa.

Recording document properties

Recording document properties allows you to jot down and keep notes to yourself — and others — regarding the purpose and content of a PowerPoint presentation. This isn't a really high-profile feature of PowerPoint, but it is useful for labeling files for future reference, particularly when you deal with lots and lots of presentations. A PowerPoint document's properties include its filename and directory, the template used to create the file, and other information you provide, such as the presentation's title, subject, author, keywords, and comments.

To examine or update a document's properties:

1. Open the file.

2. Choose File⇨Properties from the main menu.

A Properties dialog box appears.

3. Click the Summary tab to add/update file properties.

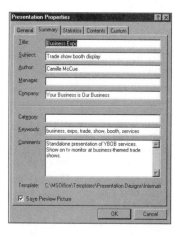

4. Click OK.

5. Choose File⇨Save to save changes.

Troubleshooting

Although you probably don't plan on your house burning down any day in the near future, you likely have taken out fire insurance nonetheless. With this same thinking in mind, you should create your own insurance for computer troubleshooting for the future. That way, when you are in crunch time, you have the knowledge to get through the crisis.

Can't find a file?

The File⇨Open command has search criteria that can help you retrieve files.

✦ **File name:** Lets you specify any portion of the filename your brain may selectively recall.

✦ **Files of type:** Allows you to specify the file type for which you are searching. This is a great option when, for example, you know that the file you seek is a Word document or an Excel spreadsheet.

✦ **Text or property:** Lets you type a piece of text and then search for all files containing that text anywhere within the presentation.

✦ **Last modified:** Allows you to specify the time frame when you most recently updated the file for which you are searching. Choices include today, yesterday, this week, last week, this month, last month, and any time.

Can't select a slide object?

One of the most annoying and commonplace PowerPoint frustrations occurs when you try to click on a slide object and you find that you can't select it, no matter what. Somewhere between scratching your head and throwing your computer against the wall, you realize the simple truth: The object resides on the slide master. Switch to the slide master view and try to select the object again.

Slide show moving too slowly?

If your slide graphics are very elaborate, you may find that an eternity passes between when you click the mouse and when you transition to the next slide. Try reformatting slide graphics in an editing program by reducing the number of colors or saving graphics images in a more compressed format to reduce file size. Move repeatedly used images in a presentation from individual slides to the slide master. Consider copying and running your presentation from your computer's hard drive to decrease access time. Performing a complete dry run of a slide show before actually conducting the presentation in front of an audience also helps.

Wondering where your video is?

Another common slide show problem involves forgetting to bundle call-to videos along with your presentation. Remember, videos are not merged with other PowerPoint elements like text and graphics — they remain as stand-alone files which play on command during the slide show. Don't call-to something that's not there! If you copy your PowerPoint file to another computer, you must copy the call-to files along with the presentation.

Saving your work in an organized manner makes finding lost videos much easier. Consistent file organization also makes it less likely you'll lose your files in the first place! It's also the key to avoiding the time-wasting chore of searching through several folders to ferret out your call-to files. *See* "Smart File Management" earlier in this part for guidance in organizing all related files into one folder.

Having presentation equipment problems?

If you are planning on presenting a sound-enhanced slide show, check that the system on which you'll be showing your show has sound capabilities. Make sure that speakers are properly connected and that they play loud enough for larger audiences to clearly hear your embedded audio.

Carefully weigh what level of display power you require to present to your intended audiences. Taking along an LCD panel with your notebook requires only that your presentation location provide an overhead projector — but LCD panels tend to be somewhat pricey and have poor color contrast. If you use one, make certain that you use high contrast colors between text and background — and kill the use of small clip art or detailed photographic images.

A scan converter that connects your notebook to a television may be the best compromise of cheap and professional, but be warned: I implore you to check — in advance — that the TV you'll be borrowing sports the necessary connections for mating with your converter. I've been caught often with a TV that has every plug except the one I need to connect my scan converter. You may need to route the scan converter through the RCA video-in jack on a VCR, then connect the VCR to the TV using an RCA-to-coaxial cable. A VHS player will not suffice, as it does not have a video-in jack – only a video-out jack. A little research ahead of time can save you a lot of headaches.

It also behooves you to take along your own cables, including extension cords and surge protectors. They're cheap and transportable, and their ready presence will make you feel better. You never know what you just might have to plug into at the other end.

And for the really paranoid among you, take along a set of over-head transparencies of your presentation. There's nothing like peace of mind!

Having printing problems?

In the event that your PowerPoint presentation poops out your printer, try investigating the following rundown of potential offenders:

✦ Check that the printer's power cord is plugged in and that the printer is turned on.

✦ Check the printer cable to ensure that it's connected to the printer port on your computer if you're using a serial or parallel connection.

✦ Check that the printer itself is set to Operate or is in on-line mode.

✦ If you're printing to a network printer, examine the printer queue to ensure that no one is tying up the printer ahead of you.

✦ Check to make sure there's plenty of paper in the printer tray and that the ink cartridge is functioning.

✦ Make sure the printer is available and listed in your Printer dialog box.

Techie Talk

action button: A clickable AutoShape that allows the presenter to perform a special action such as jumping to another location in or out of the PowerPoint slide show.

alignment: Describes how blocks of text are lined up: left, center, right, or justified. Can also describe how other objects are arranged relative to each other or relative to the entire slide.

animation: Describes how and in what sequence slide objects appear onscreen during a slide show presentation.

archiving: Saving and logically organizing PowerPoint slide shows so that they can be easily retrieved and used at a later date.

assistant: A computerized Microsoft mentor who offers help with presentation-building functions such as find, spell-check, and save. Assistants appear in their own special window and take the form of a cartoon character such as The Genius or Power Pup.

AutoContent Wizard: A quick-start option for creating a new PowerPoint presentation. Recommended for novice users who want to create a presentation with minimal effort.

AutoLayout: A slide layout which is preset with placeholders for slide objects such as the slide title, a selection of clip art, or a graph. PowerPoint asks you which AutoLayout you want to use each time you create a new slide. PowerPoint offers a wide variety of AutoLayouts to suit your slide construction needs.

AutoShape: Any of an assortment of stars, banners, callouts, and lines you draw as a single step. AutoShapes are available on the Drawing toolbar.

background: The base layer that appears behind all objects on a slide. The background may be a single color, shaded colors, a texture, or a picture. The background may be changed on a slide-by-slide basis.

blank presentation: A blank presentation possesses Slide and Title Masters devoid of background color and without artistic design elements. The only objects located on the Masters of a blank presentation are title and text placeholders.

bullet: A symbol that indicates the start of a new line or block of text on a slide.

callout: A location on a PowerPoint window or dialog box. Callouts identify or define the function of special regions on a window or dialog box, such as buttons, drop-down boxes, scrollbars, and radio buttons.

clip art: Non-photographic images.

Clip Gallery: The Microsoft collection of clip art, pictures, sounds, and videos that you can access and use for building PowerPoint slides.

clipboard: The holding pen where Windows stores the text or image that has most recently been cut or copied.

collapse: Reduces a presentation in outline view such that only slide titles are shown.

color scheme: A coordinated collection of colors you can choose for the slide background and its associated text and accents.

Common Tasks toolbar: A toolbar consisting of three of the most common presentation-building functions: New Slide, Slide Layout, and Apply Design.

copy: To use the Edit⇨Copy or Ctrl+C command to place a copy of something such as an object or a slide on the clipboard.

cut: To use the Edit➪Cut or Ctrl+X command to delete something such as an object or a slide.

datasheet: The limited function spreadsheet from which a graph is built for display on your PowerPoint slide. The datasheet consists of cells, gridlines, row and column headings, and scroll bars.

delete: To cut or otherwise obliterate the currently selected object.

document properties: Text information that accompanies your PowerPoint file and provides a description about the file. The description may include file size, a summary paragraph, and keywords.

drag: To simultaneously hold down the mouse button while rolling the mouse.

Drawing toolbar: The toolbar containing PowerPoint's drawing tools. Drawing tools include AutoShapes, Fill Color, Shadow, and others. Summon the Drawing toolbar by choosing View➪Toolbars and clicking the Drawing check box.

duplicate: Performs the same function as the two-step process of cut-and-paste.

embedded object: An object placed on a slide that was created by some program other than PowerPoint. Examples include Excel spreadsheets, sound files, movies, and organizational charts.

Equation Editor: A program that may be used to easily build mathematical expressions and equations — from simple to complex — for inclusion on your PowerPoint slides.

expand: In outline view, shows slide details that have been previously collapsed.

file format: A characteristic of a computer file that describes what program created the file, or the standard to which the file adheres (for instance, .WAV and .AU file extensions both represent music files, although they are not the same file format).

fill: To color the interior of a shape such as a polygon. Fills may be colors, textures, patterns, or pictures.

Find: To request a search for a specific word or sequence of text among your PowerPoint slides.

flip: To create the mirror image of a clip art image or other object. Flipping may be performed vertically or horizontally.

flowchart: A graphical representation of a process or series of steps that can be created using drawing tools or possibly the Org Chart program.

font: A typeface.

footer: A Master Slide object that appears positioned at the bottom of each slide in the presentation.

formatting: Typically refers to the text formatting of a text object. Can also refer to the attributes of an image, such as fill color of a clip art or shadow position of a picture.

frames: An HTML format that shows PowerPoint slides, the associated outline, and speaker notes pages simultaneously in the Web browser window.

freeform shape: A multisided shape that may contain curved sides.

Genigraphics: A third-party company that offers a service in which 35mm slides, posters, and color transparencies can be created from your PowerPoint file.

GIF: An uncompressed graphics file format. When converting PowerPoint slides to HTML for display on the web, you have an option of showing slides as GIF images.

gradient: A fill effect in which one color gently blends to white or black; or two colors gently blend with each other.

group: To attach selected objects so that they can be manipulated — resized, moved, and reformatted — as a single object.

handle: A small box that defines the edge of a selected object. Clicking and dragging the handle resizes the object.

Handout Master: The blueprint that determines how slide images will be arranged on the printout distributed to audience participants.

header: A Master Slide object that appears positioned at the top of each slide in the presentation.

hidden slide: A slide that is not displayed during a slide show.

HTML: The language in which web pages are built for display on the Internet.

hyperlink: An object, usually text, that can be clicked during a slide show to jump to another location in or out of the show.

I-beam: The cursor that appears when working inside a text box. The I-beam cursor functions the same as a word processing cursor. Also called an insertion point.

insertion point: *See* I-beam.

JPEG: A compressed graphics file format that loads more rapidly than a similar GIF file. When converting PowerPoint slides to HTML for display on the web, you have an option of showing slides as JPEG images.

justified text: Text spaced so that the left edge of the text is left-justified (flush left) and the right side of the text is right-justified (flush right).

layering: Moving a selected object in front of or behind another object.

LCD panel: A screen that attaches to your computer and displays the same onscreen images as your computer. The screen is placed atop an overhead projector so that your computer images can be displayed to an audience.

line style: Line characteristics including thickness, dash style, and arrow style.

Line style: A button on the Drawing toolbar that sets the weight (thickness) of a line.

lowercase: An option in the Change Case dialog box. When chosen, all selected text changes to lowercase letters.

macro: A recorded series of keystrokes that can be played back to simplify complex command sequences that are used repeatedly.

Master: A blueprint that defines the layout of a PowerPoint slide or printed page.

Meeting Minder: A pop-up box — accessible during a PowerPoint slide show — in which you can jot down notes and action items discussed with your audience. Meeting Minder notes may be stored for future reference.

menu bar: The bar that resides at the top of the PowerPoint window and provides basic functions such as Save, Edit, and View.

move backward: To position the selected object one layer behind its current layer.

move forward: To position the selected object one layer in front of its current layer.

move to back: To position the selected object behind all other objects on the slide.

move to front: To position the selected object in front of all other objects on the slide.

multimedia: Sound or movies that may be added to your PowerPoint slides to give them extra pizzazz.

Navigation toolbar: A group of action buttons that allow the PowerPoint user to navigate backward and forward through the presentation.

Notes Master: The master blueprint that defines the layout of your notes pages.

notes pages: Blocks of text (such as speaker comments and supporting notes) that accompany a PowerPoint slide but do not appear onscreen during a formal presentation.

Notes Pages view: The view that shows how your notes pages appear. A notes page typically features a slide thumbnail at the top of the page, followed by a text box filled with speaker notes or other text at the bottom of the page.

object: An element on a slide. Can contain text, clip art, charts, and other types of graphics.

on-the-fly: A PowerPoint feature in which spelling is checked as you type. Possible misspellings are underlined.

Outline view: Displays the text from your PowerPoint slides in the form of an outline. Can be accompanied by a thumbnail of the Slide view. One of two construction modes for building PowerPoint presentations (the other is Slide view).

Pack and Go Wizard: Packages a PowerPoint presentation, its fonts, and the PowerPoint Viewer so that the presentation can be viewed on a computer that does not have PowerPoint installed.

paste: To use the Edit⇨Paste or Ctrl+V command to add a copied object to a slide or a copied slide to a presentation.

picture: A non-clip-art image. An image composed of rows and columns of colored dots called pixels that combine to form a complete photograph-like figure.

pixel: A small, colored dot that combines with other small, colored dots to create an image.

placeholder: A message such as Click to add title that shows the location where text can be typed.

polygon: A multisided shape with sides composed of straight lines.

PowerPoint viewer: A program that allows you to run a PowerPoint slide show on a computer that does not have the PowerPoint program installed.

PPT: The filename extension of a PowerPoint presentation.

presentation: Most simply, a PowerPoint slide show. The presentation may also be considered the complete set of PowerPoint slides, speaker notes, and audience handouts.

Presentation Designs tab: The location of a collection of PowerPoint templates that features elegant styles devoid of specific content.

Presentations tab: The location of a collection of PowerPoint templates that features elegant styles paired with presentation content.

recolor: To selectively change the line and fill colors of any part of a clip art image.

redo: To reapply the keystroke most recently undone.

regroup: To group a collection of formerly grouped objects that have been ungrouped. Regroup requires that you select only a single object from the former group.

Rehearsal dialog box: Allows you to time and record how long it takes to display each slide during a PowerPoint slide show.

replace: To substitute new text for text retrieved during a Find search.

resize: To shrink, enlarge, or adjust the proportions of a selected object.

rotate: To spin a clip art image or other object around a central axis. Rotation may be clockwise or counterclockwise.

ruler: A measuring tool that may be toggled on and off for the purpose of positioning and aligning slide objects.

Save as HTML Wizard: A feature that allows the conversion of your PowerPoint presentation to a web-based presentation for online viewing.

scroll bar: A strip along the right or bottom side of the PowerPoint window. Pressing a scroll bar's arrows (marking the ends of the bar) or dragging the little square tab on the bar causes different parts of the window to come into view.

select: To click on an object so that its handles appear.

semi-transparent: A color treatment that allows you to make lines and fills partially see-through.

sentence case: An option in the Change Case dialog box. When selected, it capitalizes the first letter of the first word in the selected sentences.

serif: A font characterized by fancy tails that drape off the ends of the letters. A common example is Times.

shadow: To add a depth effect to text or other objects by creating the illusion that the objects cast shadows. You may change the position and color of a shadow.

slide: A single screen of information in a PowerPoint presentation. Slides may be presented as computer images, overhead transparencies, or 35mm slides.

slide layout: *See* AutoLayout.

Slide Master: The blueprint that indicates the template and object positioning for all slides that follow in the presentation.

Slide Show view: Displays slides one by one on your computer screen. The presentation mode of PowerPoint.

Slide Sorter view: Displays a screenful of small thumbnails of your PowerPoint slides. Viewing slides in Slide Sorter is similar to viewing a collection of 35mm slides on a light table.

Slide view: Displays a single slide on your computer screen, accompanied by PowerPoint toolbars that may be used to create and edit objects on the slide. One of two construction modes for building PowerPoint presentations (the other is Outline view).

spell-checking: Checking the spelling of words on your PowerPoint slides or notes pages against a standard or custom dictionary. Spell-checking may be on-the-fly or after-the-fact.

spreadsheet: An electronic ledger program such as Excel.

Standard toolbar: The toolbar where buttons common to Office 97 (and many other programs) are located. Standard toolbar buttons include New, Open, Save, Print, and others.

Status bar: A bar positioned near the bottom of the PowerPoint window that shows the number of the current slide, the total number of slides in the presentation, and the name of the presentation template.

style checker: A tool that automatically checks your presentation for correct spelling, consistent punctuation and capitalization, and readability of text size.

summary slide: A slide created automatically from the titles of all other slides in the presentation.

template: A design scheme you select when building a new PowerPoint presentation. The template prescribes colors, fonts, background designs, and artistic elements of the Slide and Title Masters.

text box: A box that resides on a PowerPoint slide and is reserved for typing and editing text. The text box may be moved, by clicking and dragging, and it may be resized by adjusting its sizing handles.

Text formatting toolbar: The toolbar where all text formatting buttons are found. This is where you select text fonts, point size, colors, and other text attributes.

theme elements: Text and objects placed on the Slide and Title Master so that they appear on every slide. Theme elements might include a company logo or trademark.

thumbnail sketch: A miniature window that shows a scaled-down version of how the window appears in its regular size. PowerPoint frequently shows thumbnail sketches of slides as little windows about the size of four postage stamps.

Title bar: The strip at the top of the window where the program name (Microsoft PowerPoint) and the presentation name appear.

title case: An option in the Change Case dialog box. When selected, it capitalizes the first letter of each word in the selection.

Title Master: The blueprint that indicates the template and object positioning for the title slide of a presentation.

toggle case: An option in the Change Case dialog box. When selected, it changes all selected uppercase letters to lowercase and vice versa.

toolbar: A collection of buttons that perform related functions.

transition: The method by which one PowerPoint slide is removed, causing the next slide to appear. Transitions include Dissolve, Fade through Black, Barn Door Open, and others.

transparencies: A low-tech option for outputting and displaying your PowerPoint slides.

undo: To reverse the action accomplished by the most recently applied keystroke or menu selection.

ungroup: To detach a grouped object into its component objects.

uppercase: An option in the Change Case dialog box. When selected, it changes all selected text to capital letters.

view: How you look at your presentation while working in PowerPoint. You have five options: Slide view, Outline view, Notes Pages view, and Slide Sorter view.

wizard: A program that provides step-by-step guidance in performing certain multistep PowerPoint functions. PowerPoint wizards include AutoContent, Genigraphics, Pack and Go, and Save as HTML.

WordArt: A special program that creates cool, three-dimensional words for use on your PowerPoint slides.

zoom: To adjust the viewing magnification of your PowerPoint slides. Viewing at 100% zoom displays slides at their true size.

Index

S

U

V

W

YOUR ONLINE RESOURCE

WWW.DUMMIES.COM

Discover Dummies™ Online!

The *Dummies* Web Site is your fun and friendly online resource for the latest information about ...*For Dummies*® books on all your favorite topics. From cars to computers, wine to Windows, and investing to the Internet, we've got a shelf full of ...*For Dummies* books waiting for you!

Ten Fun and Useful Things You Can Do at www.dummies.com

1. Register this book and win!
2. Find and buy the ...*For Dummies* books you want online.
3. Get ten great *Dummies Tips*™ every week.
4. Chat with your favorite ...*For Dummies* authors.
5. Subscribe free to *The Dummies Dispatch*™ newsletter.
6. Enter our sweepstakes and win cool stuff.
7. Send a free cartoon postcard to a friend.
8. Download free software.
9. Sample a book before you buy.
10. Talk to us. Make comments, ask questions, and get answers!

Jump online to these ten fun and useful things at
http://www.dummies.com/10useful

SURF THE NET

WWW.DUMMIES.COM

For other technology titles from IDG Books Worldwide, go to
www.idgbooks.com

Not online yet? It's easy to get started with *The Internet For Dummies*,® 5th Edition, or *Dummies 101*®: *The Internet For Windows*® *98,* available at local retailers everywhere.

IDG
BOOKS
WORLDWIDE

Find other ...*For Dummies* books on these topics:
Business • Careers • Databases • Food & Beverages • Games • Gardening • Graphics
Hardware • Health & Fitness • Internet and the World Wide Web • Networking • Office Suites
Operating Systems • Personal Finance • Pets • Programming • Recreation • Sports
Spreadsheets • Teacher Resources • Test Prep • Word Processing

IDG BOOKS WORLDWIDE BOOK REGISTRATION

We want to hear from you!

Visit **http://my2cents.dummies.com** to register this book and tell us how you liked it!

- Get entered in our monthly prize giveaway.
- Give us feedback about this book — tell us what you like best, what you like least, or maybe what you'd like to ask the author and us to change!
- Let us know any other *...For Dummies*® topics that interest you.

Your feedback helps us determine what books to publish, tells us what coverage to add as we revise our books, and lets us know whether we're meeting your needs as a *...For Dummies* reader. You're our most valuable resource, and what you have to say is important to us!

Not on the Web yet? It's easy to get started with *Dummies 101*®: *The Internet For Windows*® *98* or *The Internet For Dummies*,® 5th Edition, at local retailers everywhere.

Or let us know what you think by sending us a letter at the following address:

...For Dummies Book Registration
Dummies Press
7260 Shadeland Station, Suite 100
Indianapolis, IN 46256-3945
Fax 317-596-5498

BESTSELLING
BOOK SERIES
FROM IDG